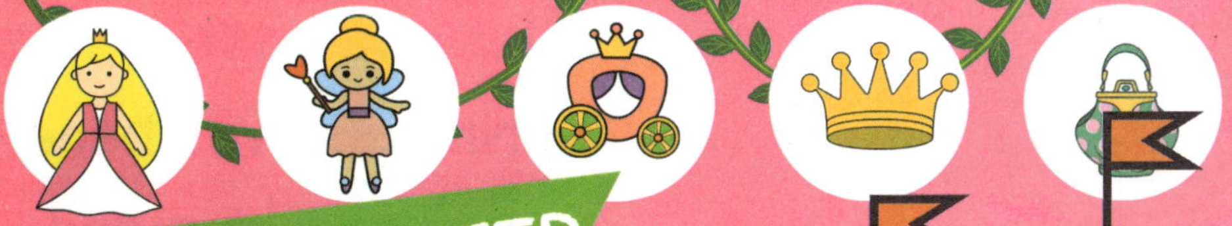

STEP BY STEP

HOW TO DRAW Princess

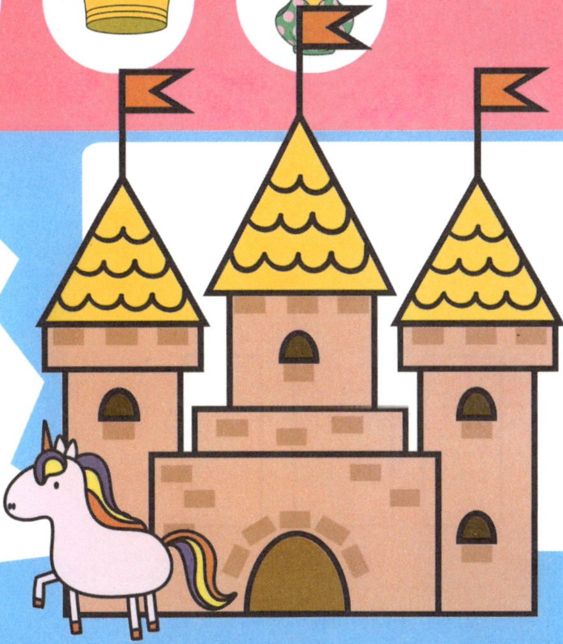

Easy steps to draw and colour for kids

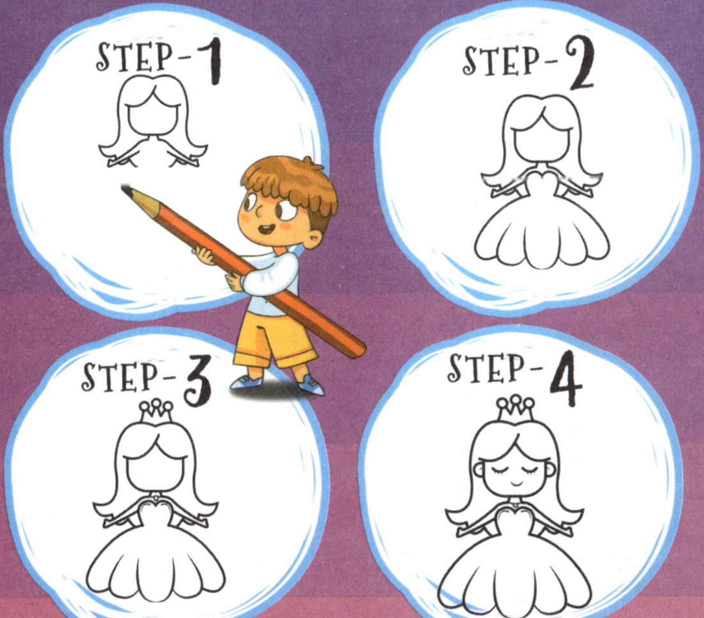

STEP-1

STEP-2

STEP-3

STEP-4

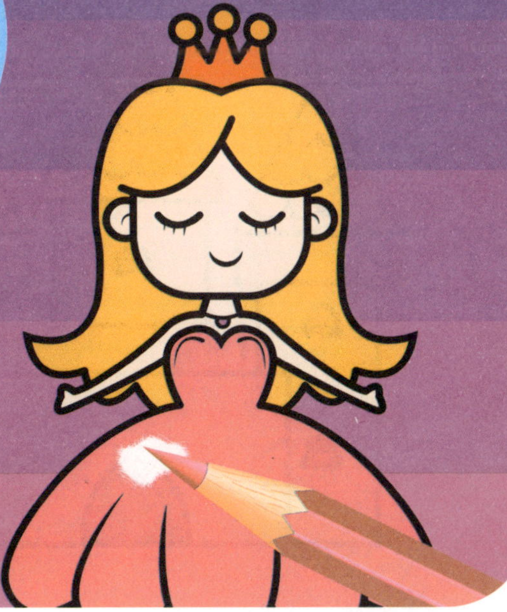

CASTLE

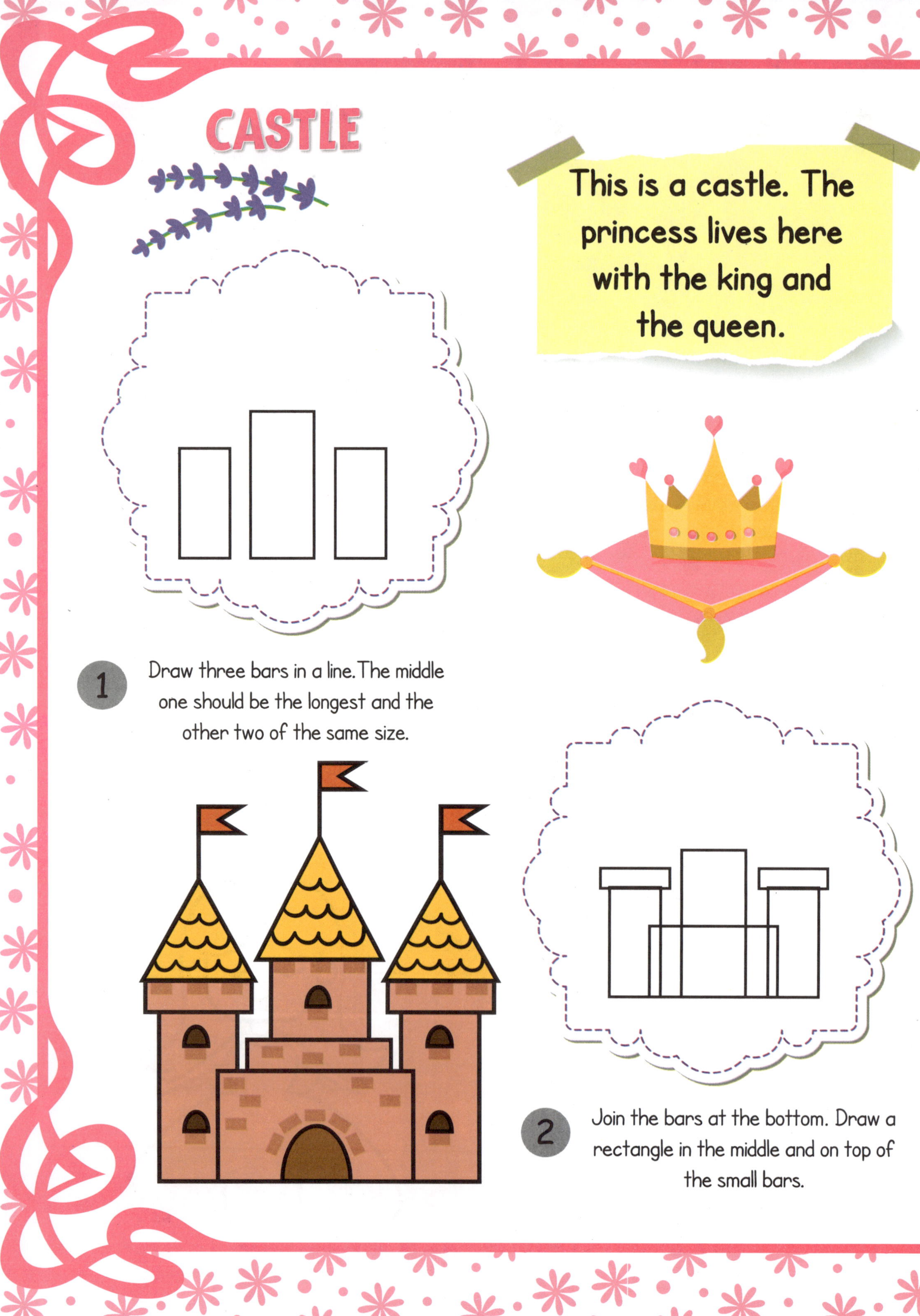

This is a castle. The princess lives here with the king and the queen.

1 Draw three bars in a line. The middle one should be the longest and the other two of the same size.

2 Join the bars at the bottom. Draw a rectangle in the middle and on top of the small bars.

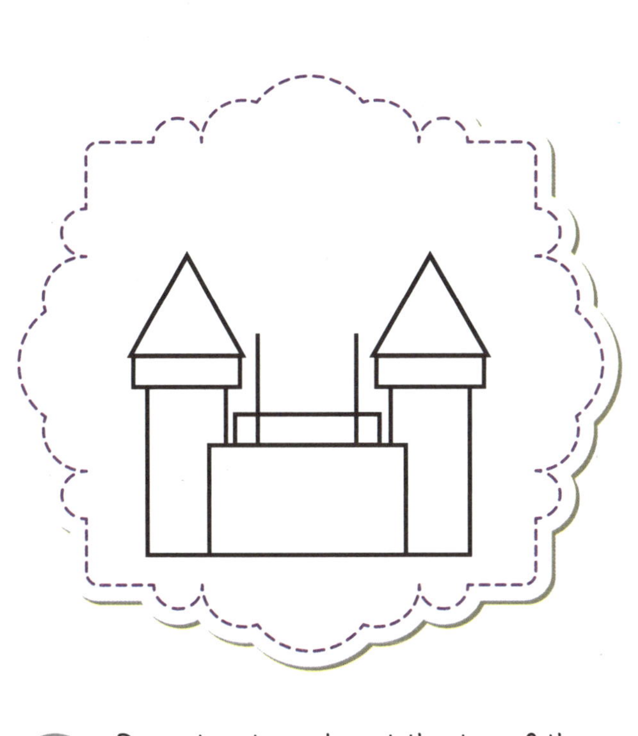

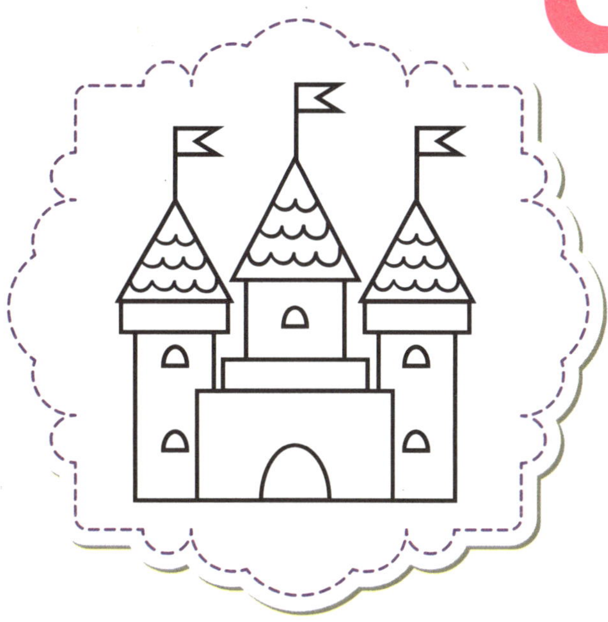

3 Draw two triangles at the top of the smaller bars. Erase unwanted lines.

4 Draw designs and flags on the bars. Make curve shapes for windows and a door.

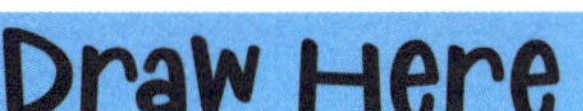

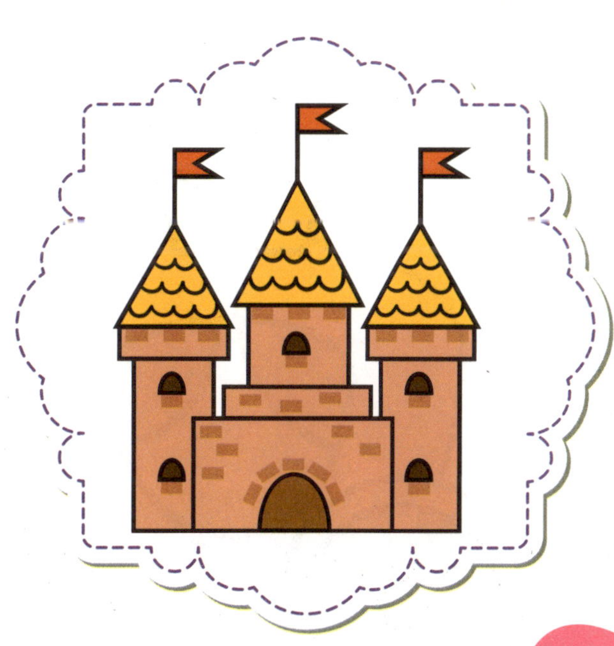

CARRIAGE

This is a royal carriage. It's used by the king and his family.

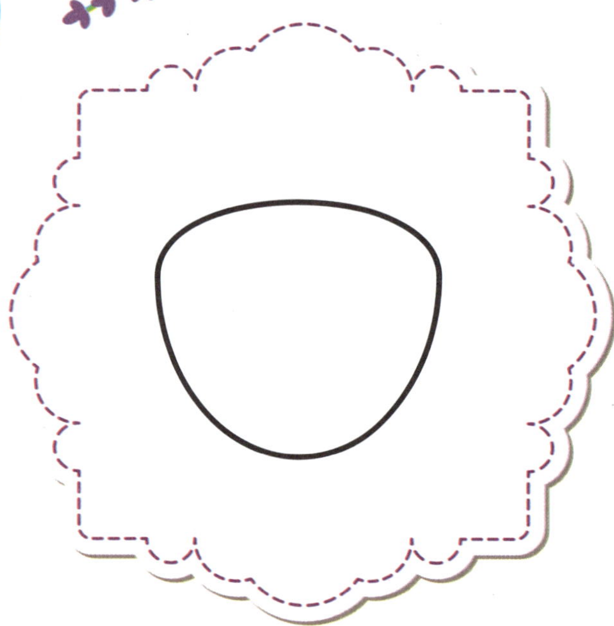

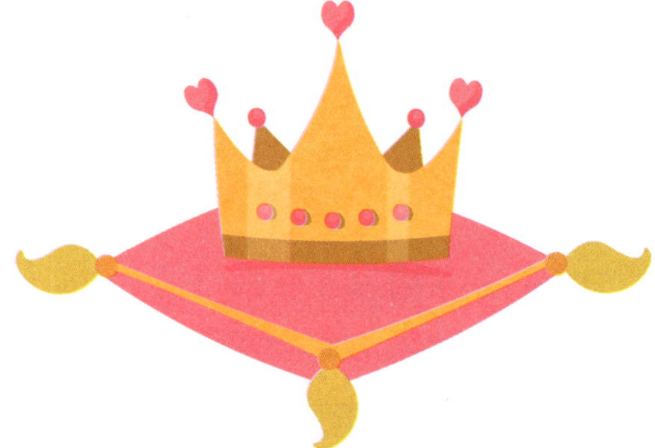

1 Draw a "C" shape and join it from above. Make sure to keep the ends curved.

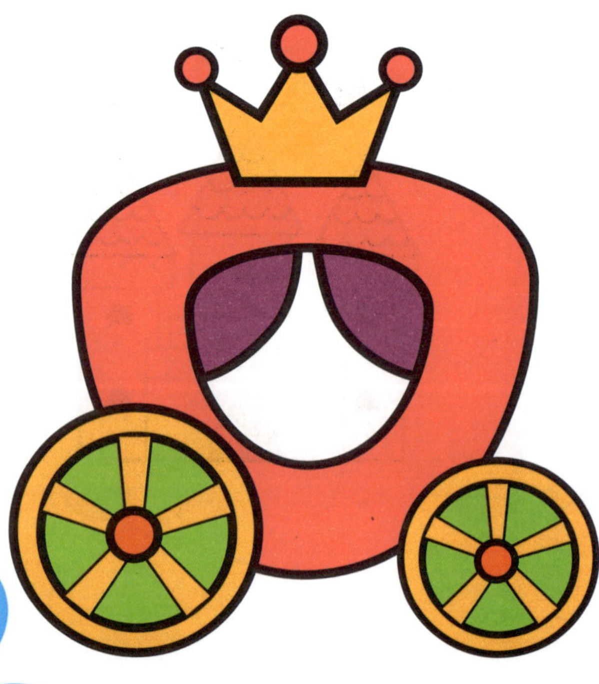

2 Copy the shape in the middle. Draw a crown at the top and two circles for wheels.

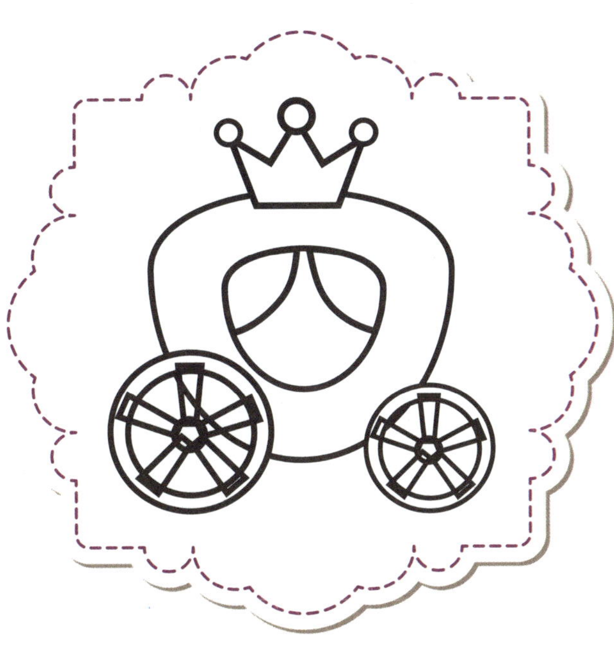

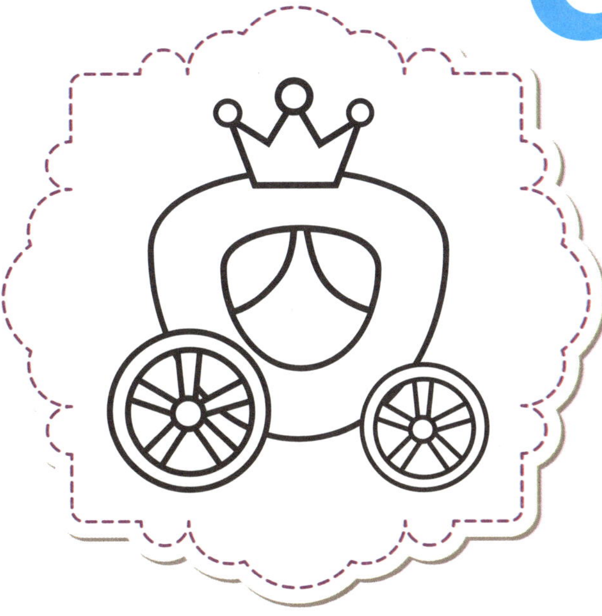

3 Draw circles on the crown and two curves for the curtains. Draw the spokes of the wheels.

4 Erase unwanted lines and colour as shown below.

Draw Here

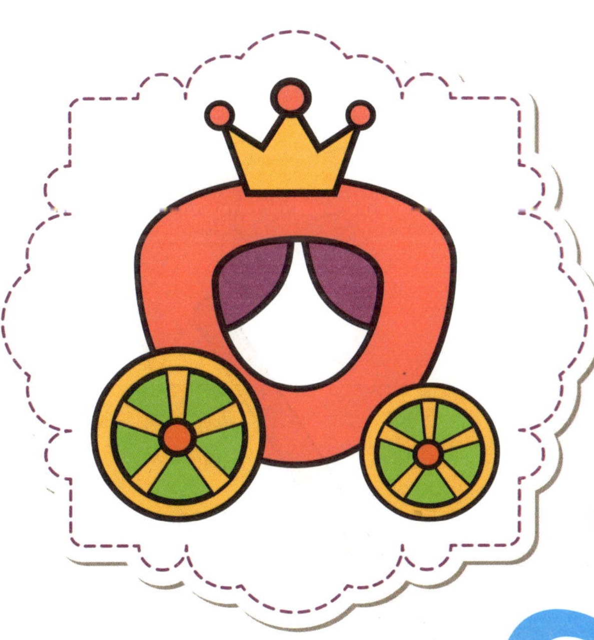

MAGIC WAND

This is a magic wand. Magicians use it to do magic.

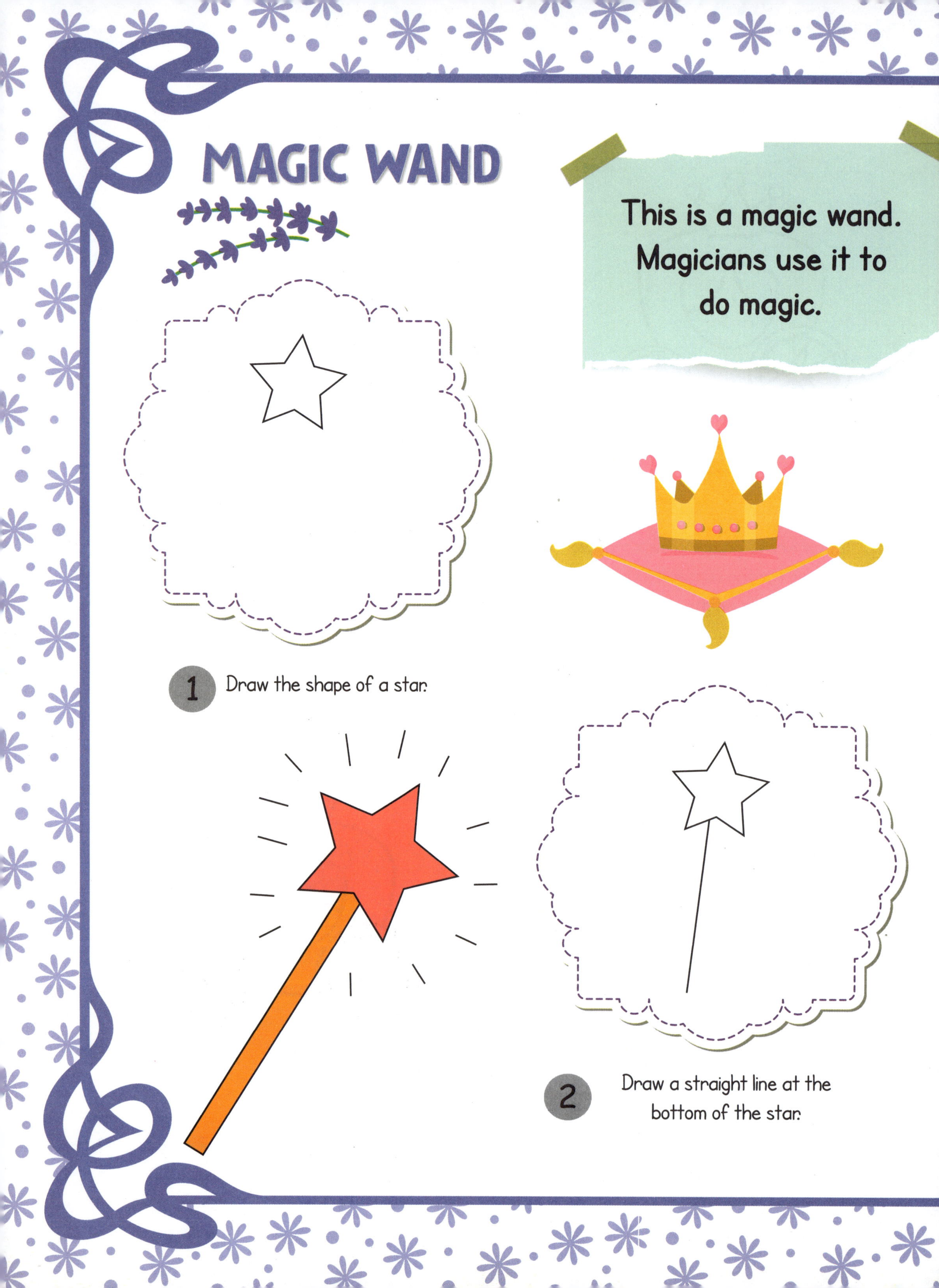

1 Draw the shape of a star.

2 Draw a straight line at the bottom of the star.

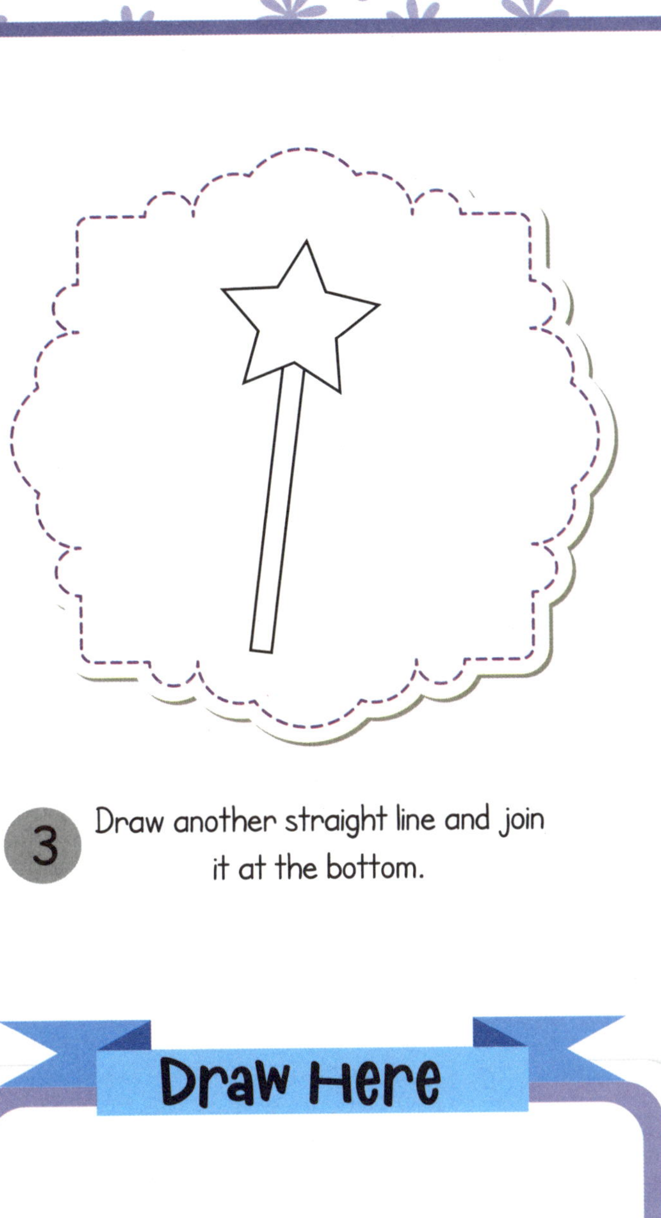

3 Draw another straight line and join it at the bottom.

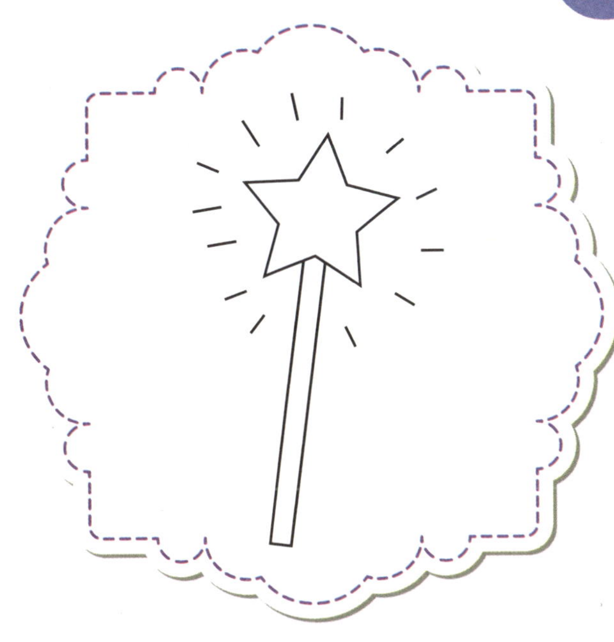

4 Draw small, straight lines all around the star. Colour to finish.

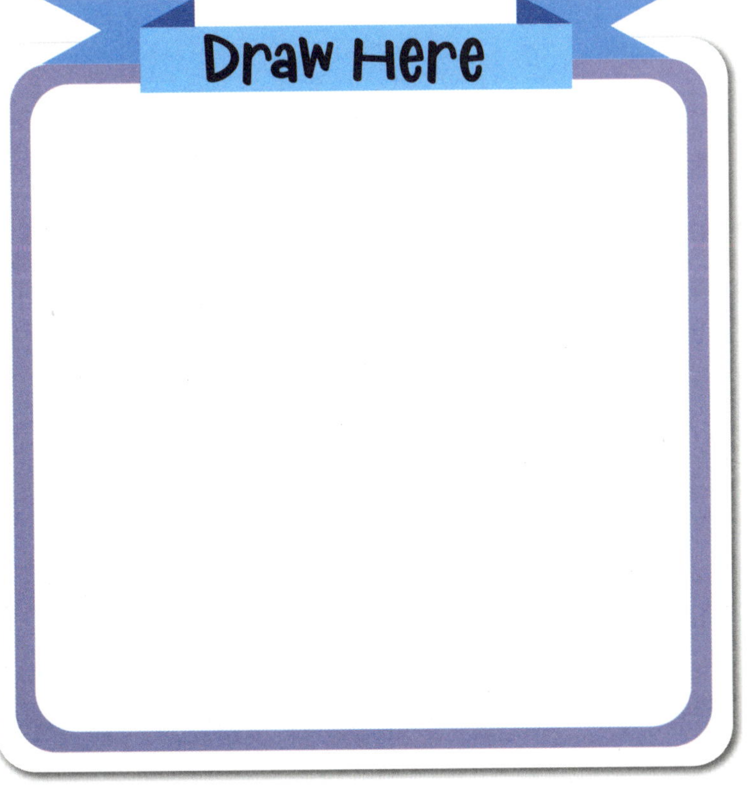

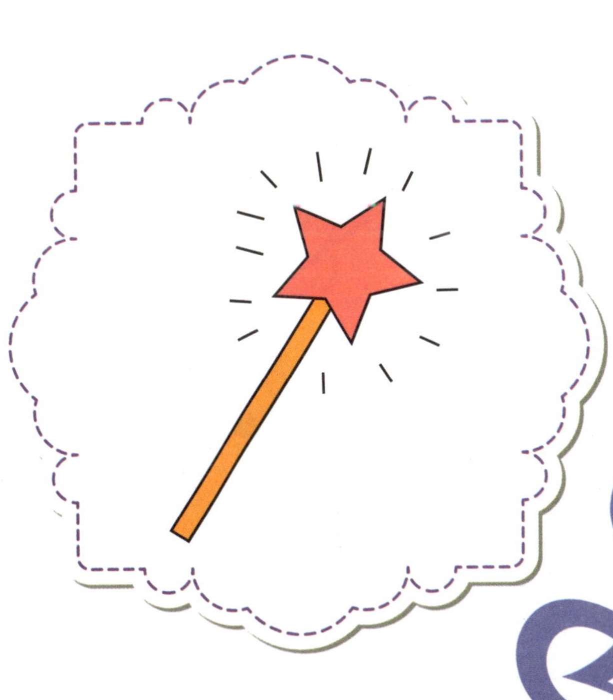

DOLL

This is a doll.
It's the princess'
favourite toy.

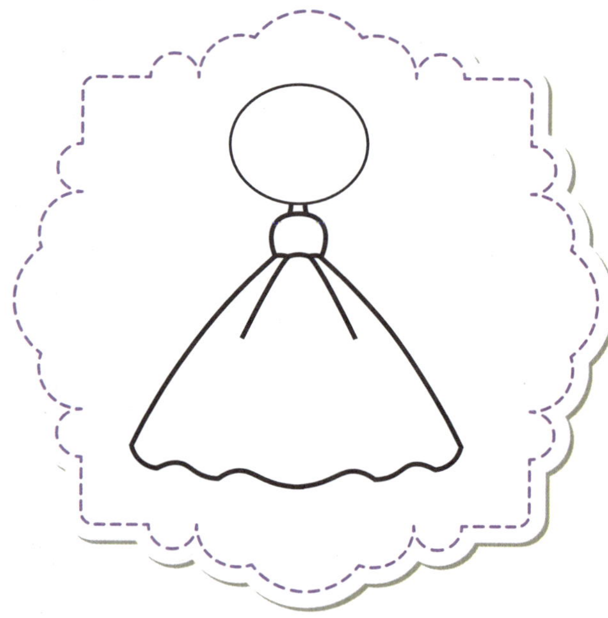

1 Draw a circle for the head. Make a neck and an upper body. For the gown, draw two lines at the bottom.

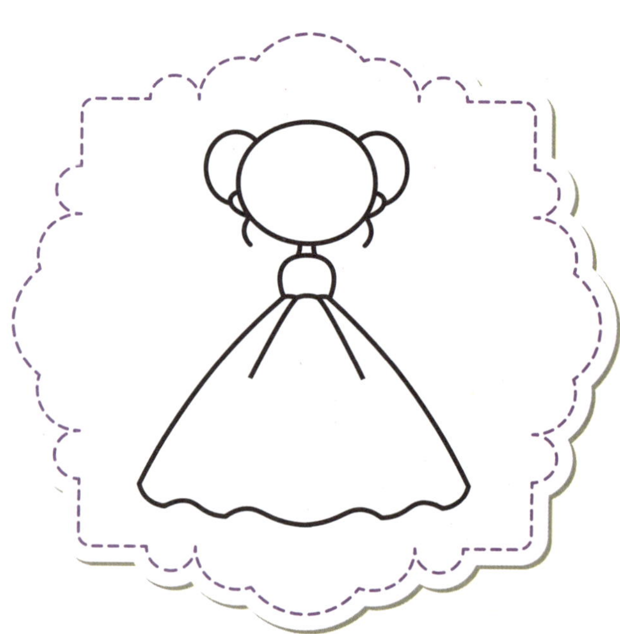

2 On the head, draw two curves for buns. Divide small spaces for ears and make two curves for earrings.

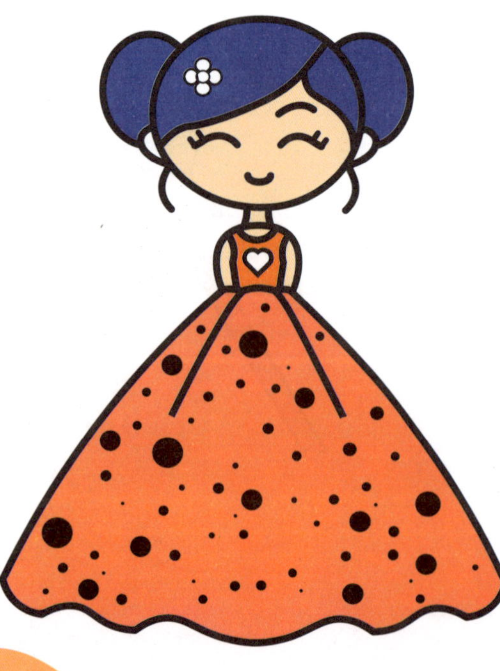

3 On the upper body, make a design and divide the sides to make arms.

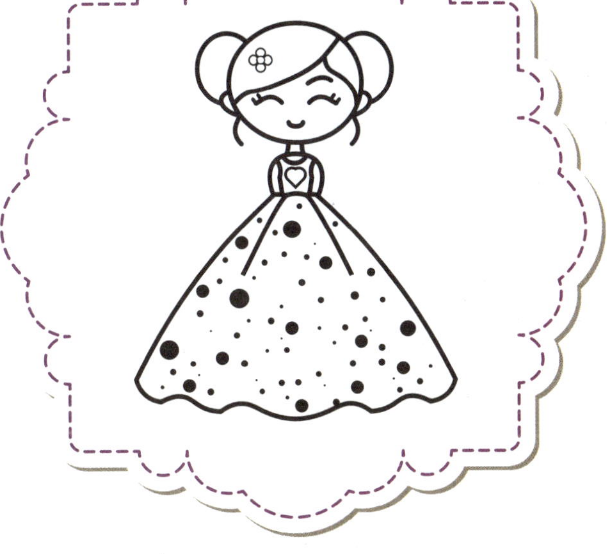

4 Make a flower on the hair for a hairclip. Draw circles on the gown. Colour to complete.

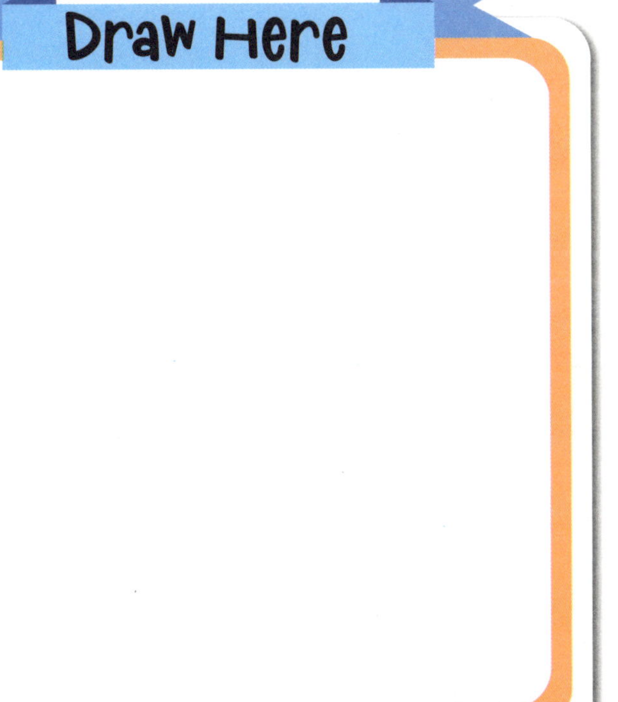

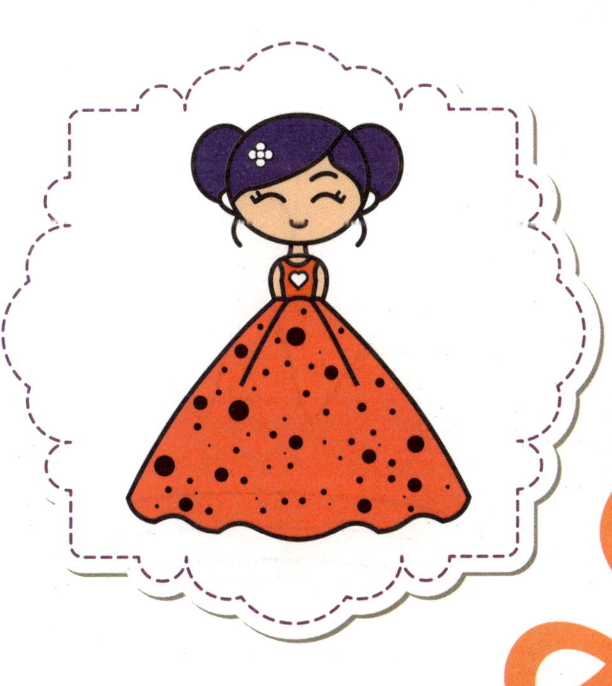

CROWN

This is a crown. The king or queen wear it on their head.

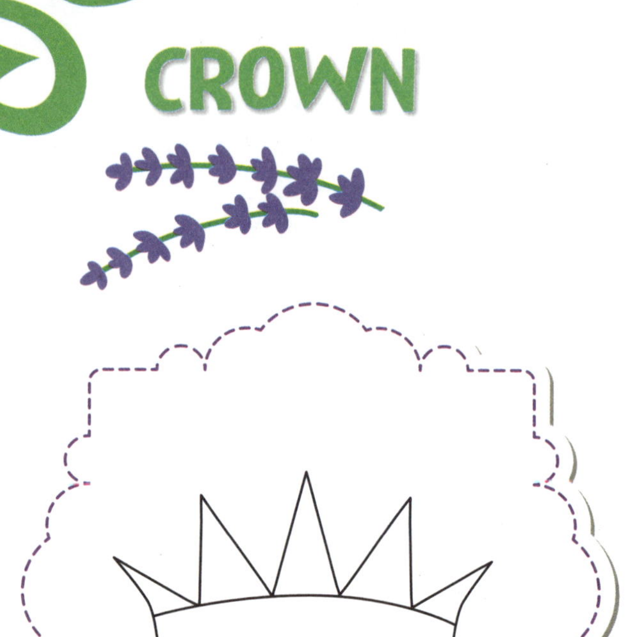

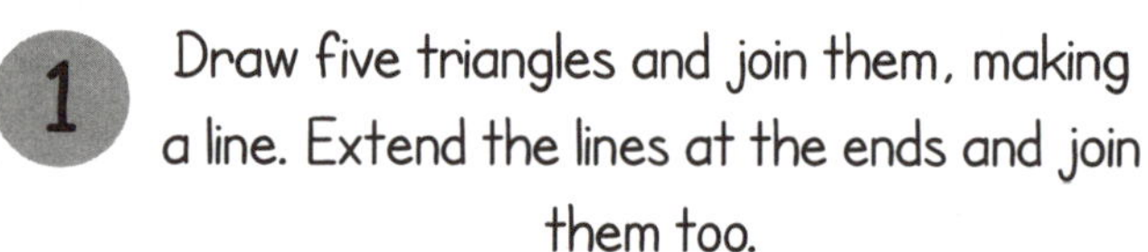

1 Draw five triangles and join them, making a line. Extend the lines at the ends and join them too.

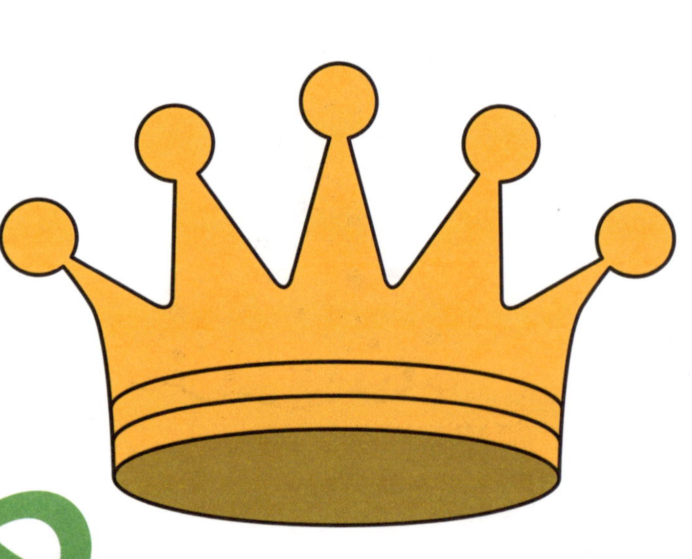

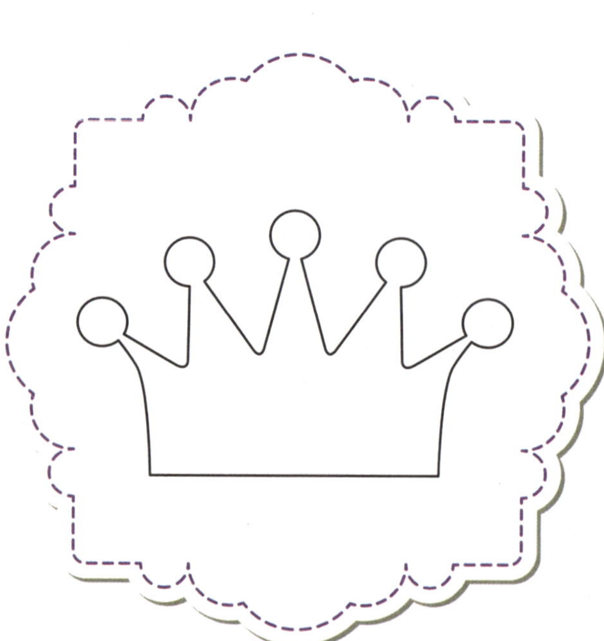

2 Draw circles at the top of the triangles. Erase unwanted lines.

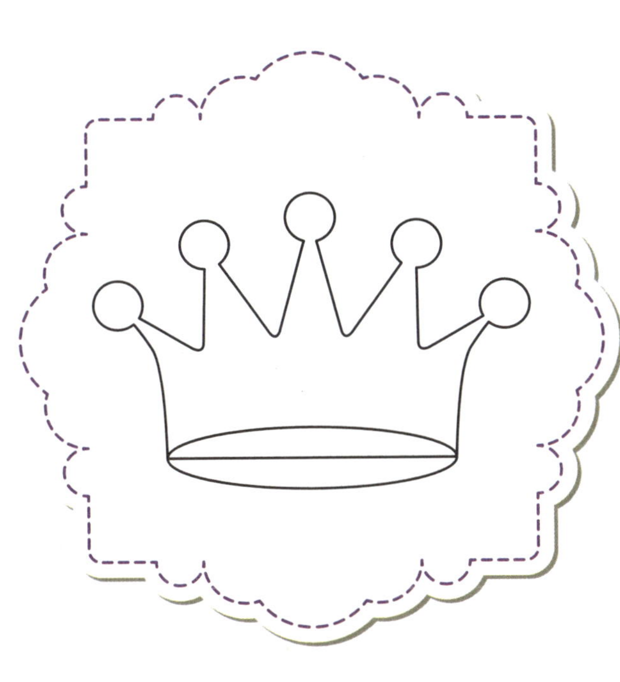

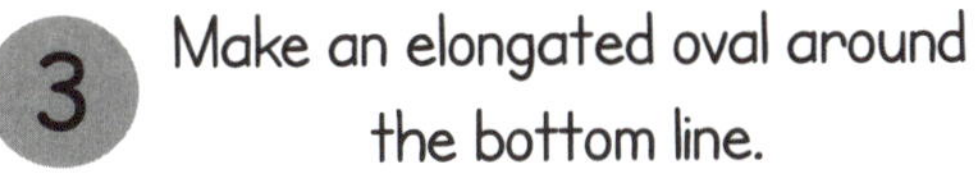

3 Make an elongated oval around the bottom line.

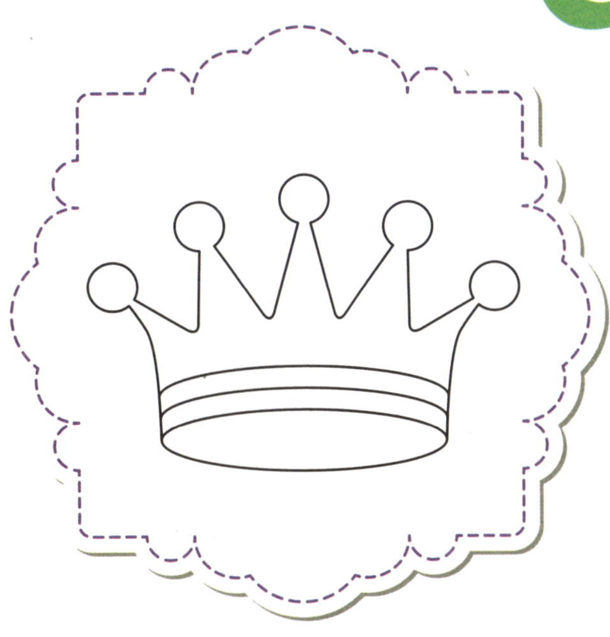

4 Erase the unwanted line. Draw three curved lines above the oval shape.

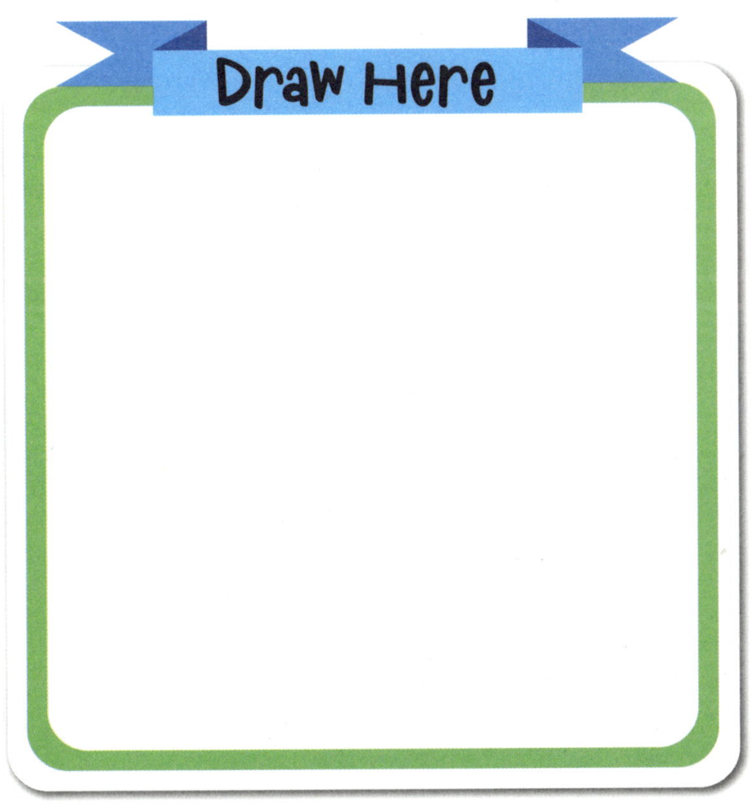

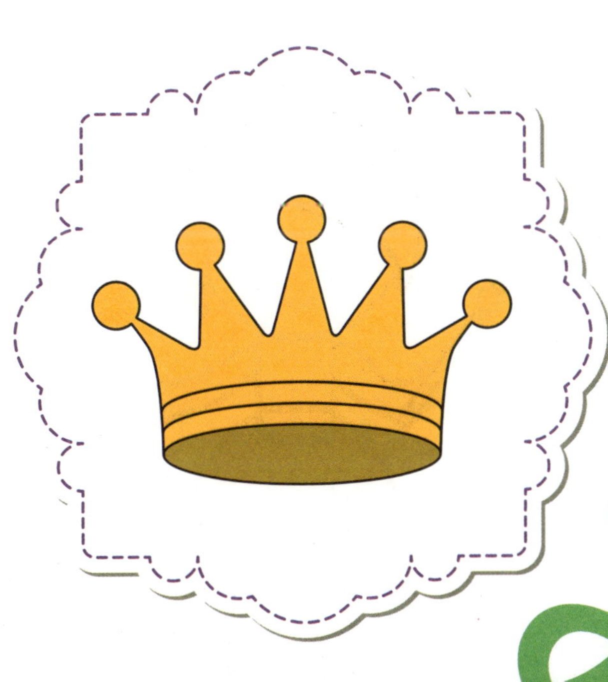

MAGICAL PRINCESS

This is a magical princess. A magical princess has magical powers.

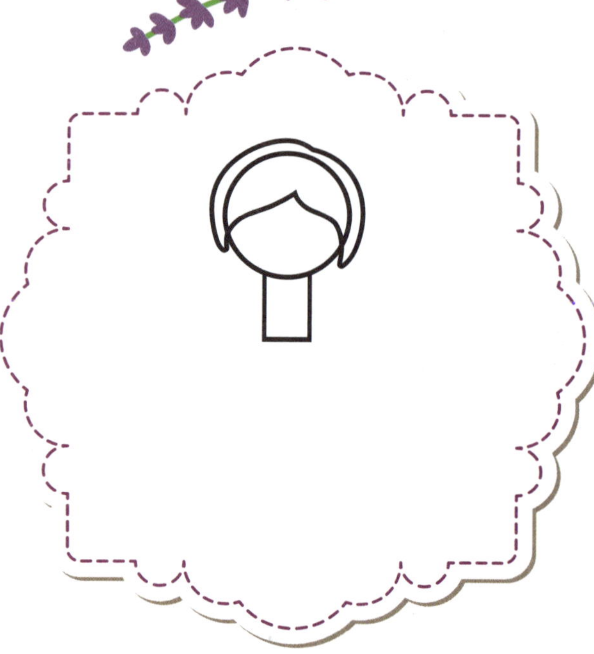

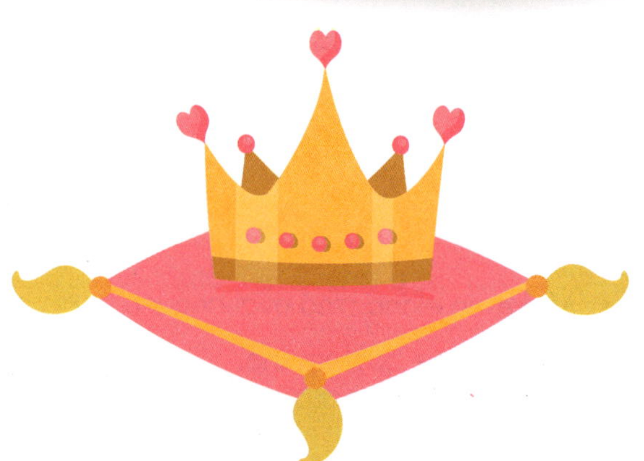

1 Draw a circle for the head. Draw hair and a cylindrical shape for the upper body.

2 Draw arms on both sides of the upper body and a gown.

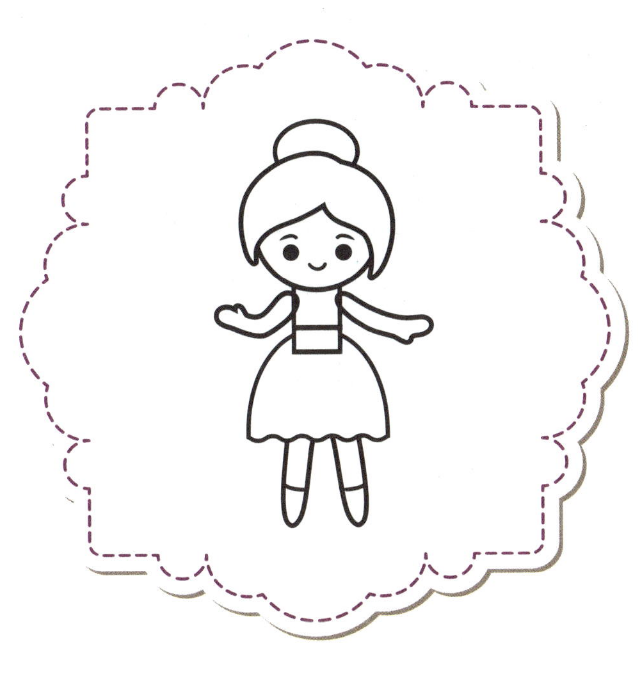

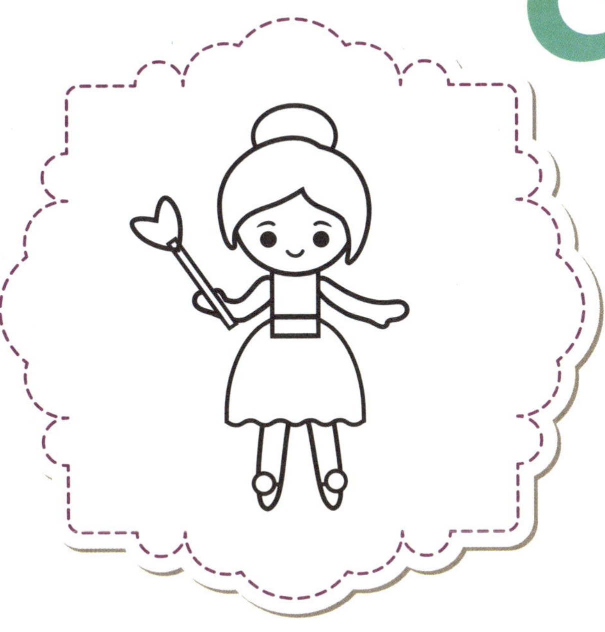

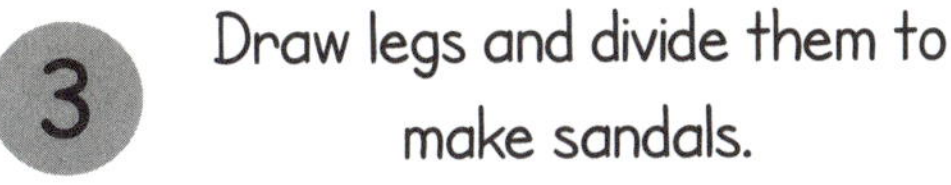

3 Draw legs and divide them to make sandals.

4 Draw a magical wand and the princess' sandals. Colour to complete.

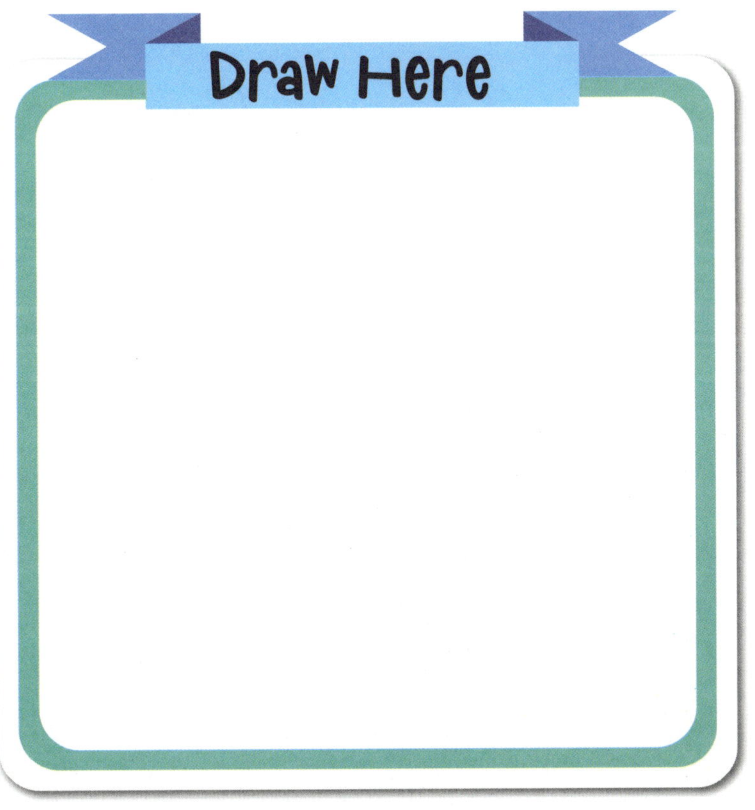

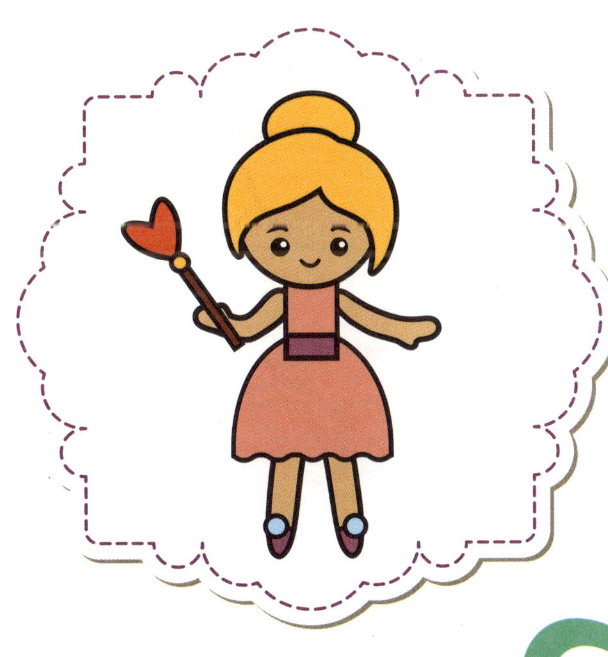

PRINCESS

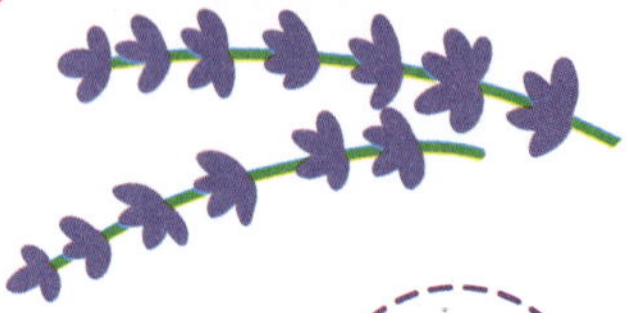

This is a princess. She lives in a castle with the king and the queen.

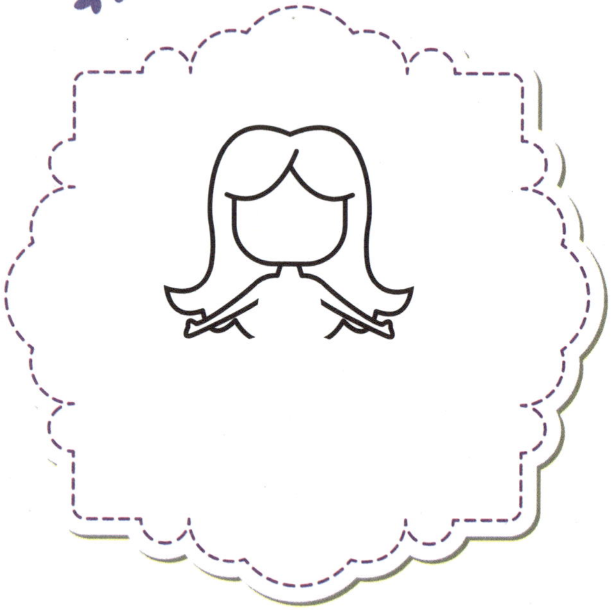

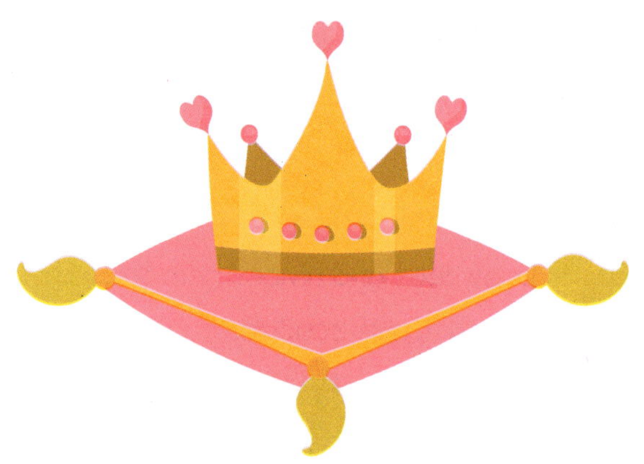

1 Draw the hair, face, upper body and arms.

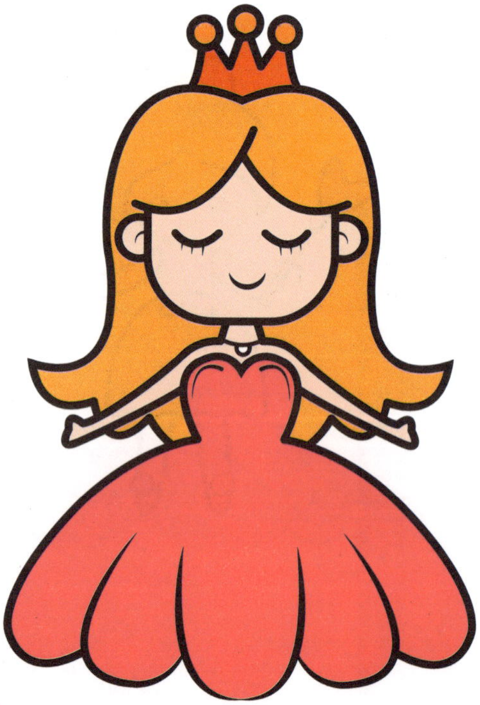

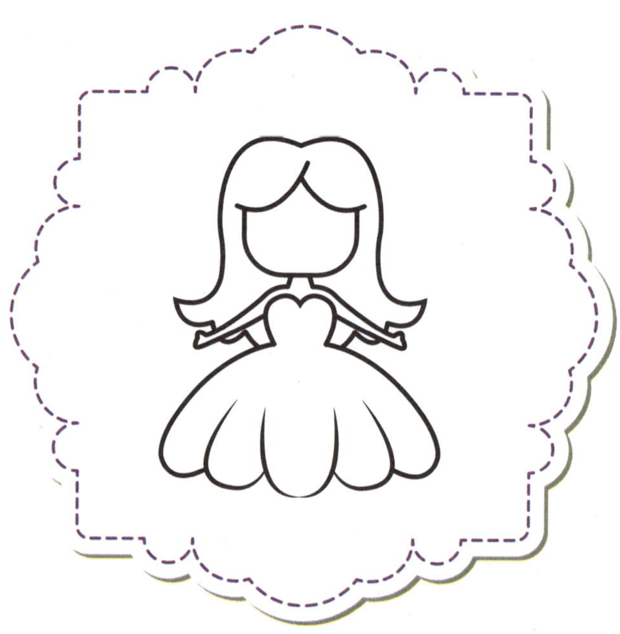

2 Draw the princess' gown, making it curved at the bottom.

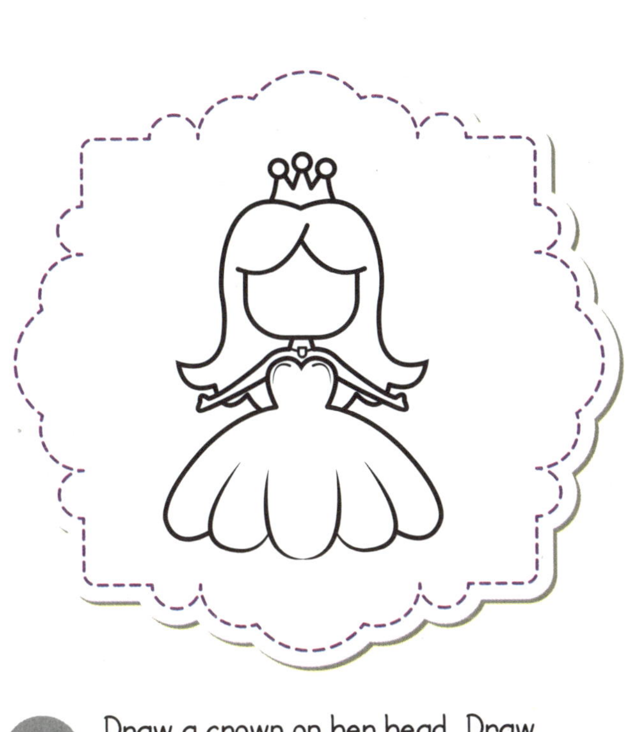

3 Draw a crown on her head. Draw a necklace and fine lines on the upper body.

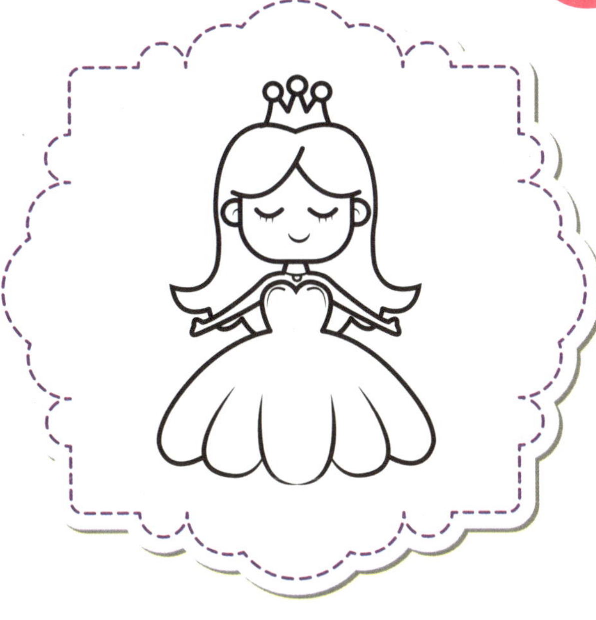

4 Draw ears, eyes and a mouth. Colour to complete.

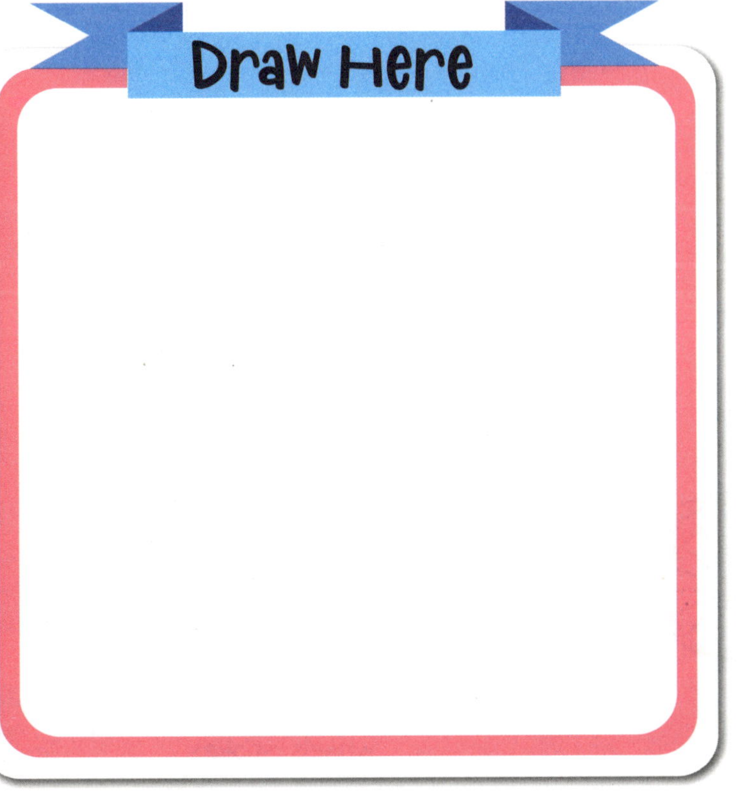

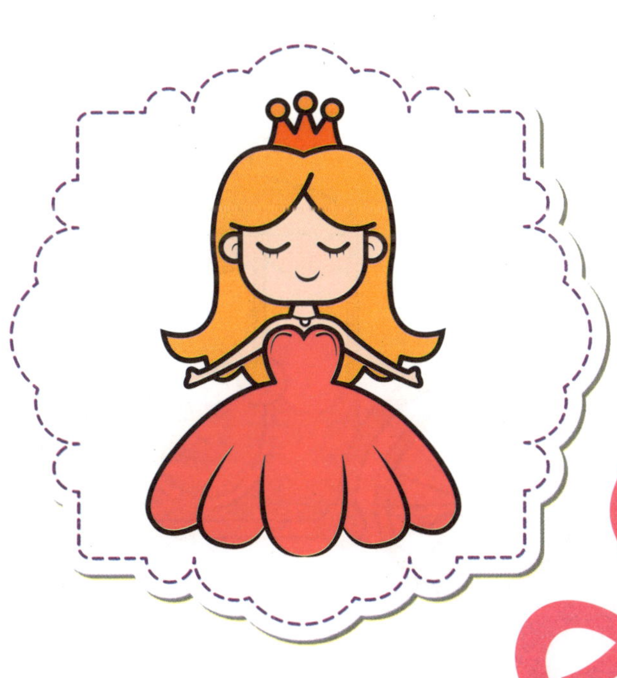

CHARIOT

This is a chariot.
It is used for
royal processions.

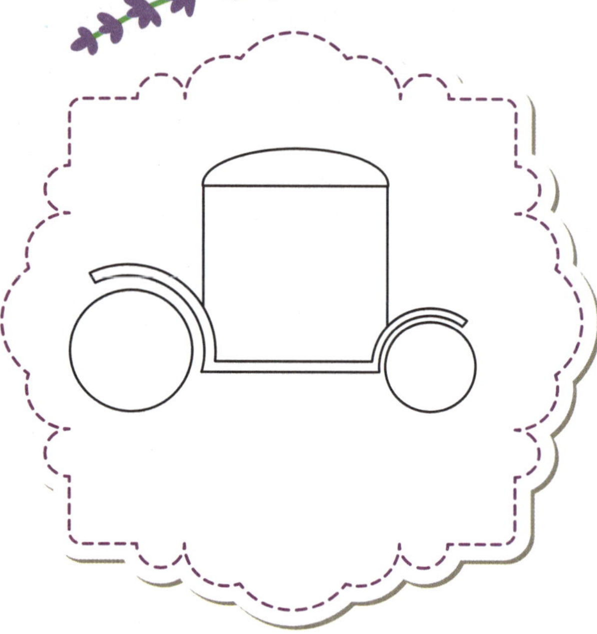

1 Draw two circles, one big and the other small, for the wheels and a square shape for the seating. Curve it at the top. Draw the wheels' mudguard.

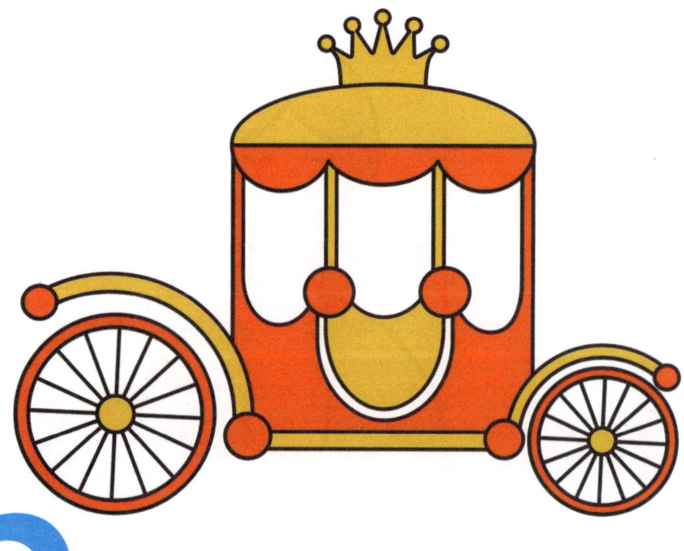

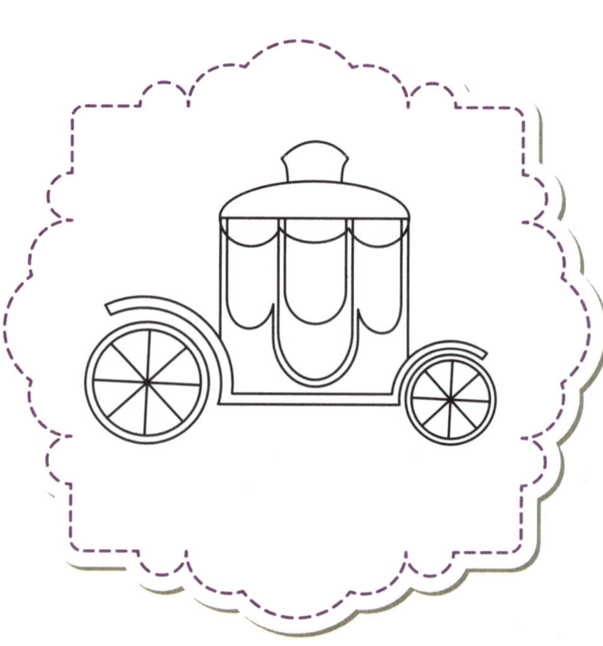

2 Draw the top of the chariot. Draw designs to make curtains. Make the wheels' spokes.

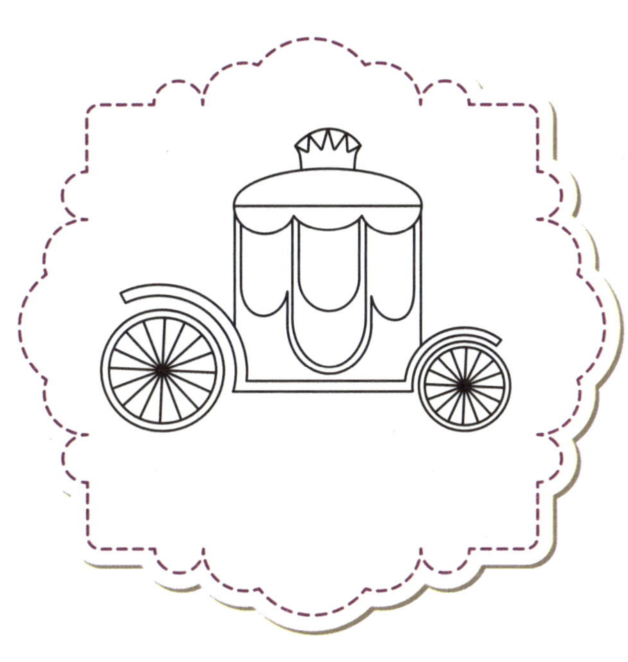

3 Draw a crown at the top of the chariot.

4 Draw circles on the door and over the wheels' mudguards. Colour to complete.

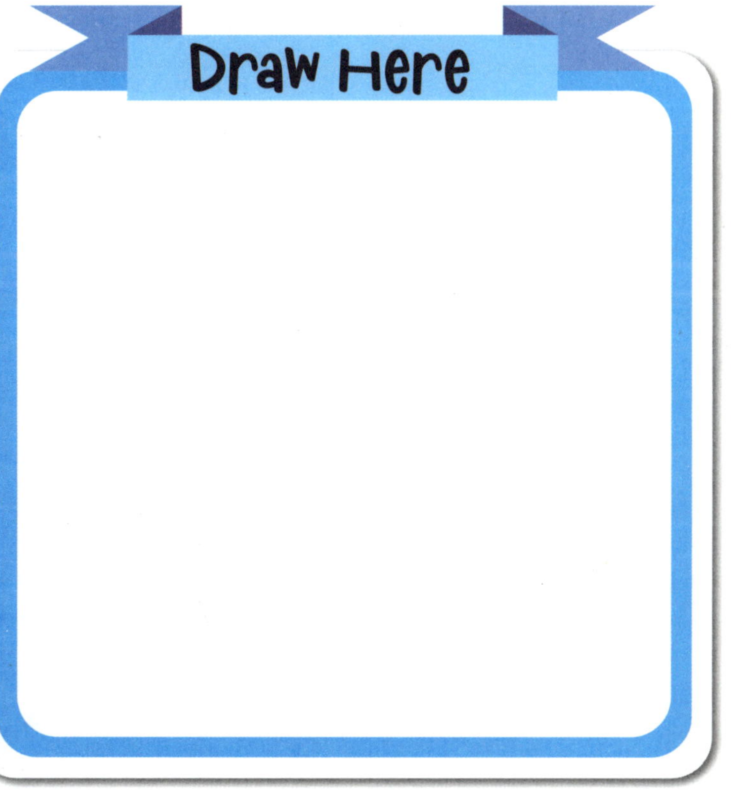

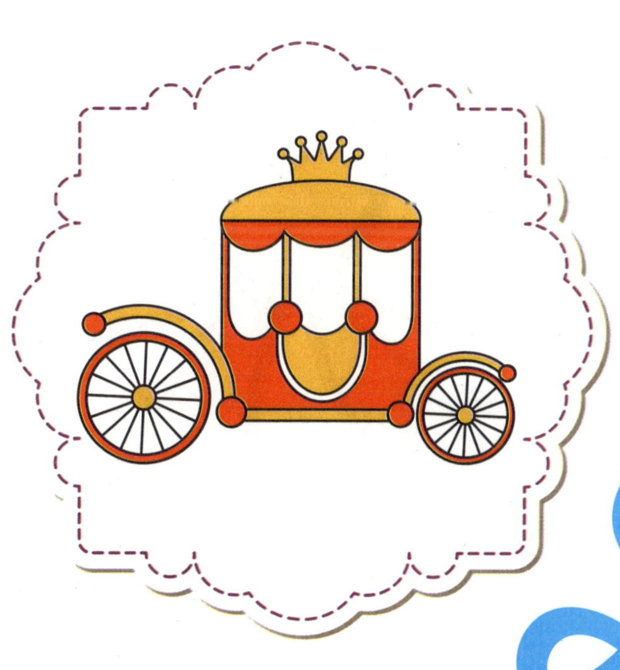

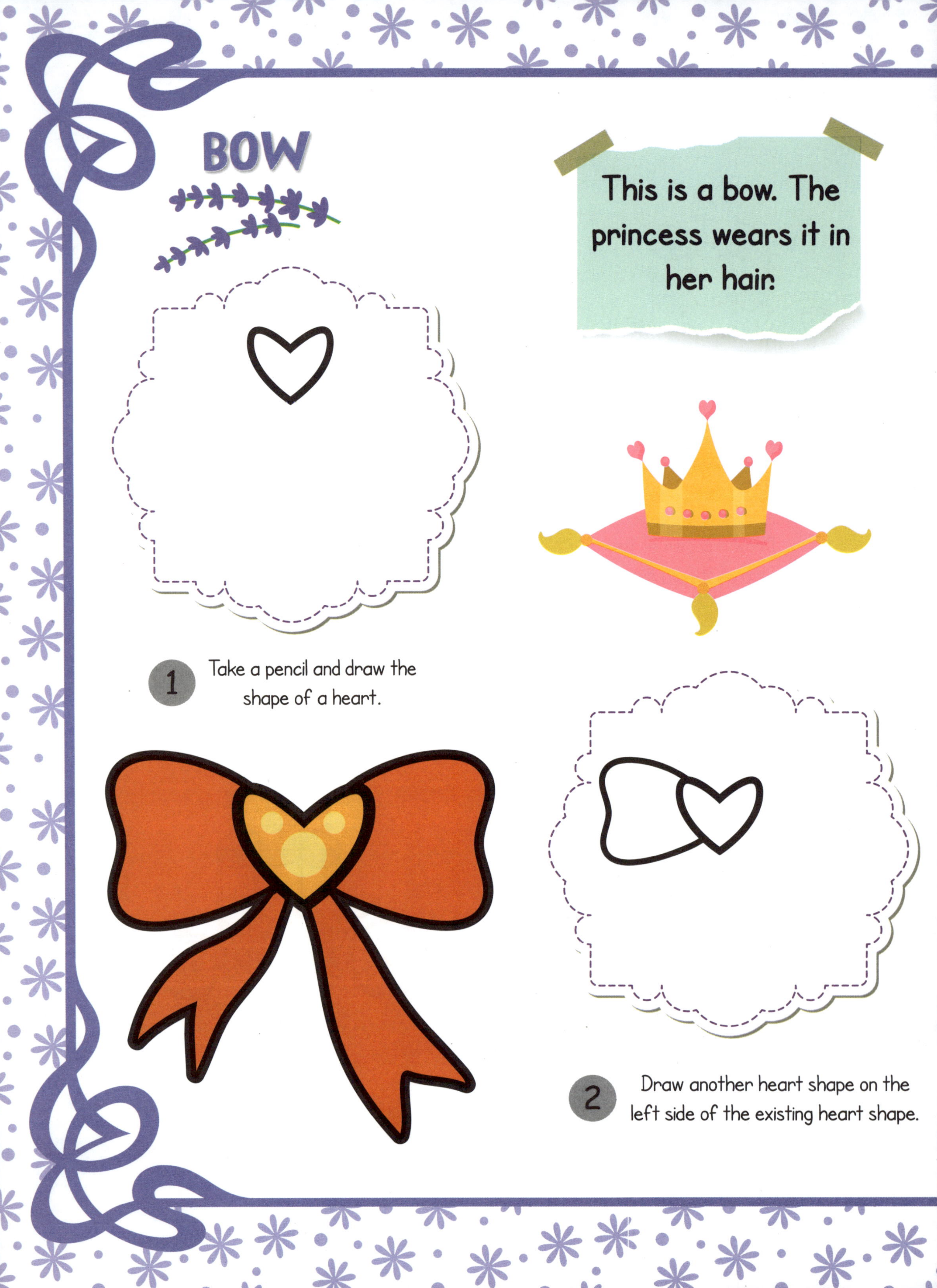

BOW

This is a bow. The princess wears it in her hair.

1 Take a pencil and draw the shape of a heart.

2 Draw another heart shape on the left side of the existing heart shape.

3 Draw a similar heart shape on the right side too.

4 Draw two ribbons at the bottom and colour it.

PRINCESS ARUBA

This is a princess. Her name is Aruba.

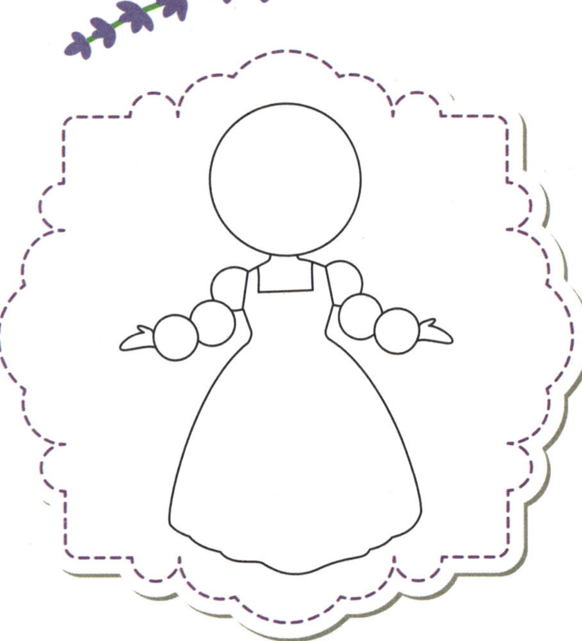

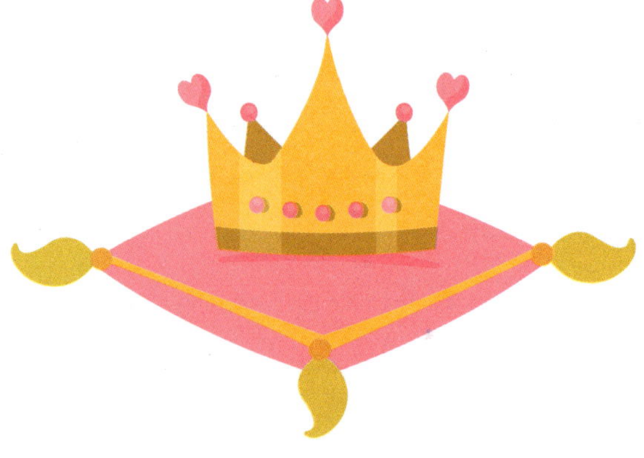

1 Draw a circle for the head. Make three circles on each side of the body for arms. Make a neck and body.

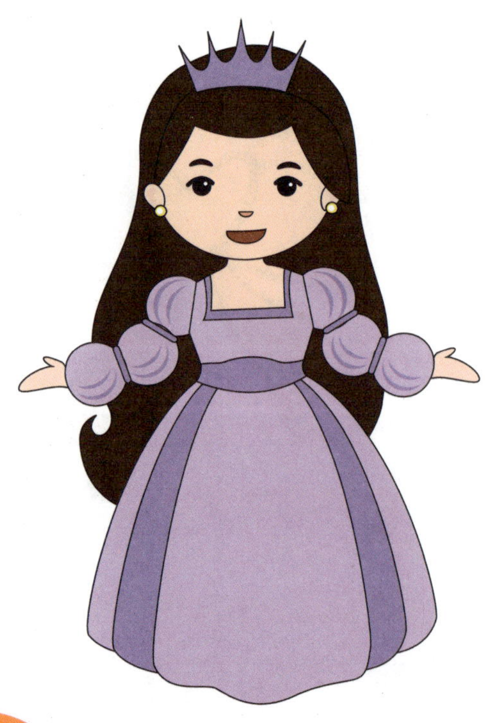

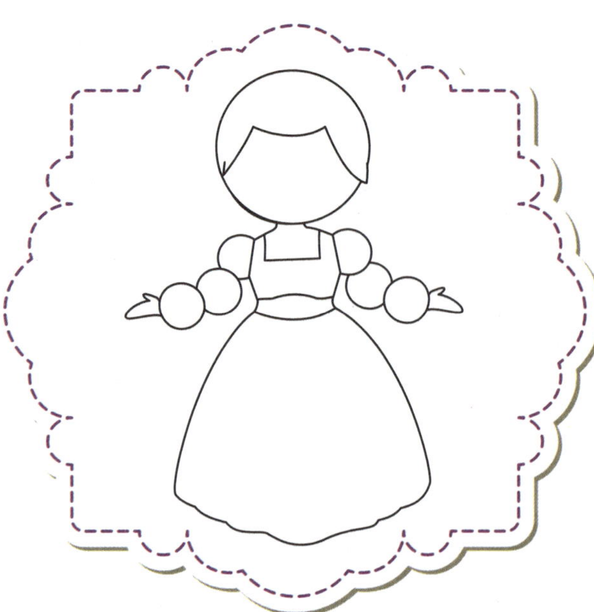

2 Draw the outline of her hair and also draw her belt.

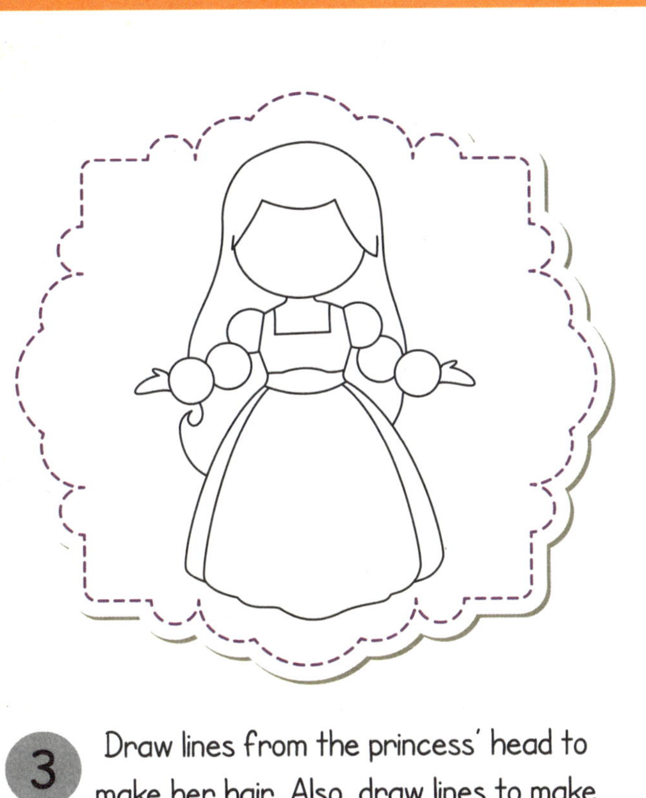

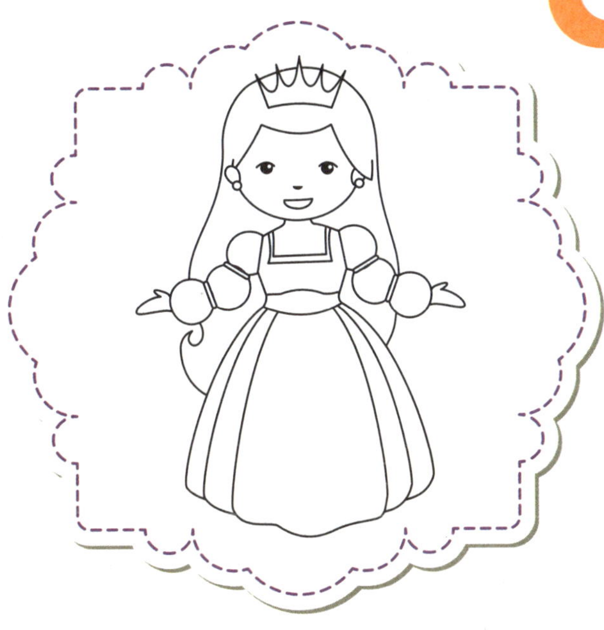

3 Draw lines from the princess' head to make her hair. Also, draw lines to make the gown's design.

4 Make a crown, ears, eyes, nose and mouth. Colour to complete.

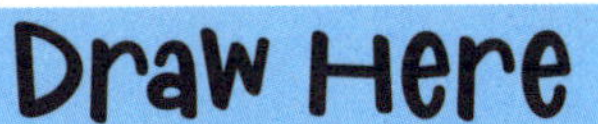

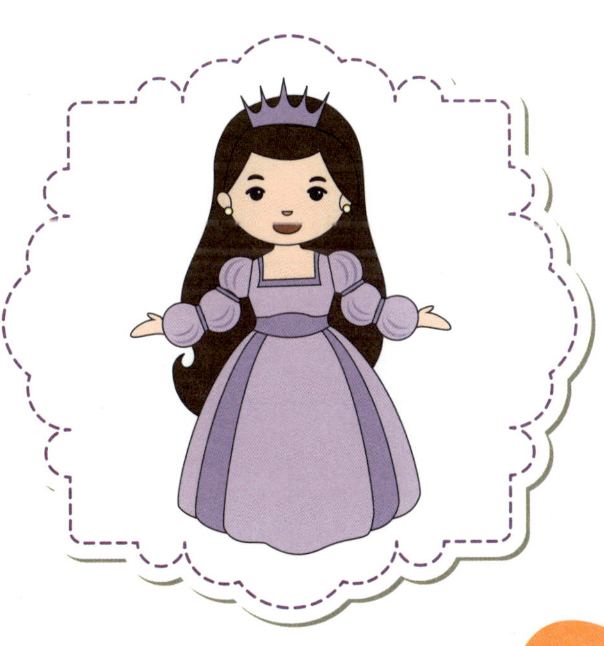

FORT

This is a fort. It has high walls to protect itself from enemies.

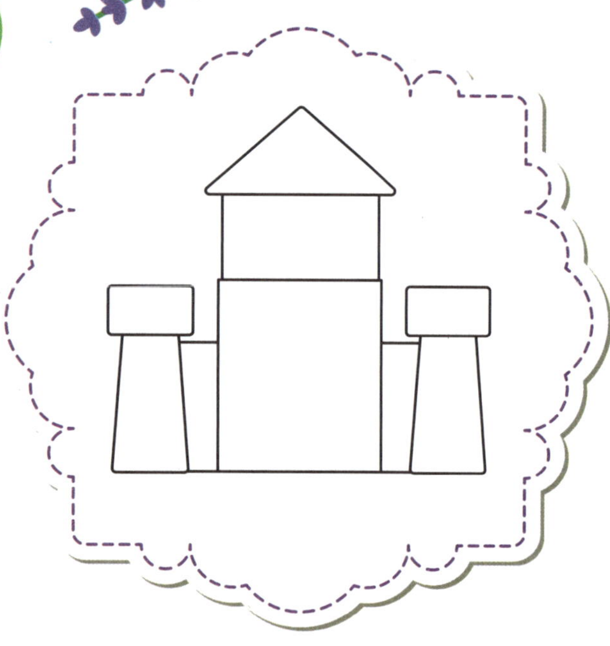

1 Draw a rectangle and divide it in two. Add a triangle to make the top. On both sides of the rectangle, make shapes of the walls.

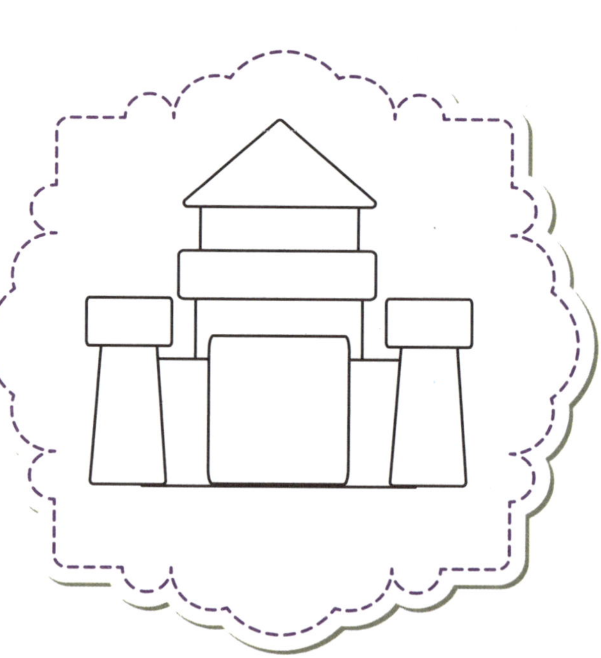

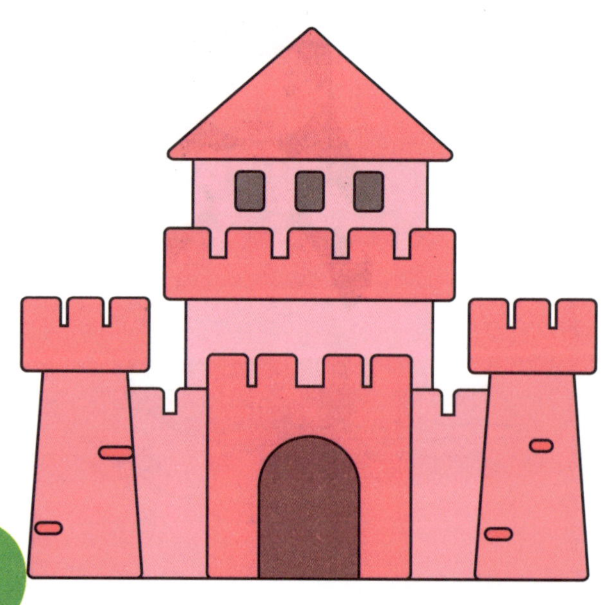

2 Draw various brick-shaped designs to make the terrace of the fort.

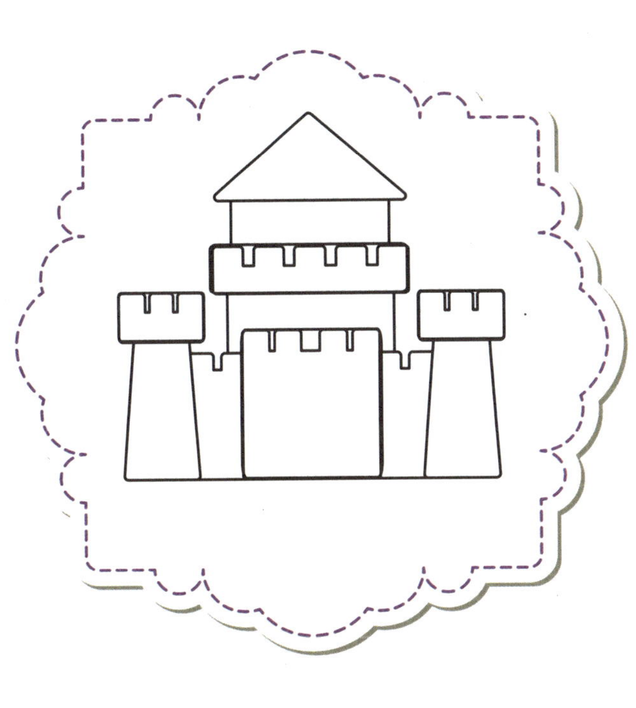

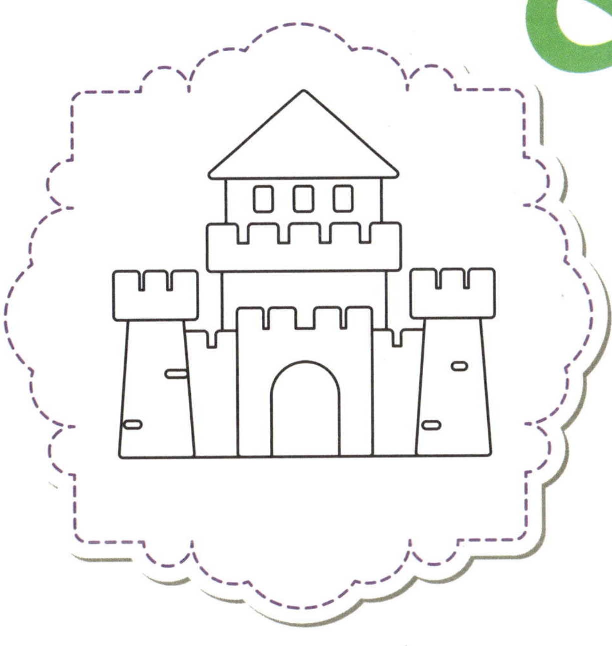

3 Make zig-zag patterns on the wall for the design.

4 Draw windows and a door. Colour to complete the fort.

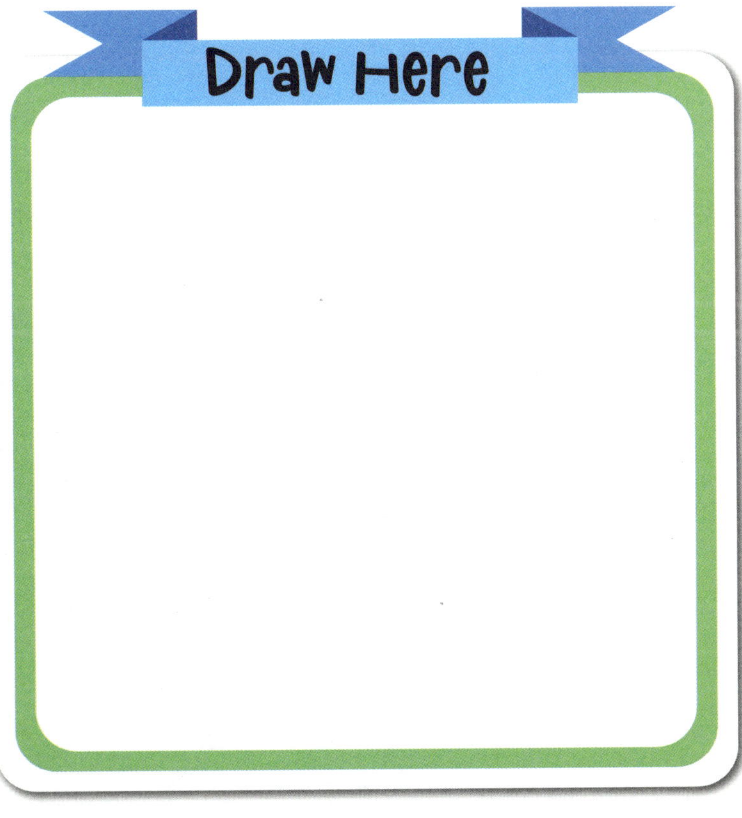

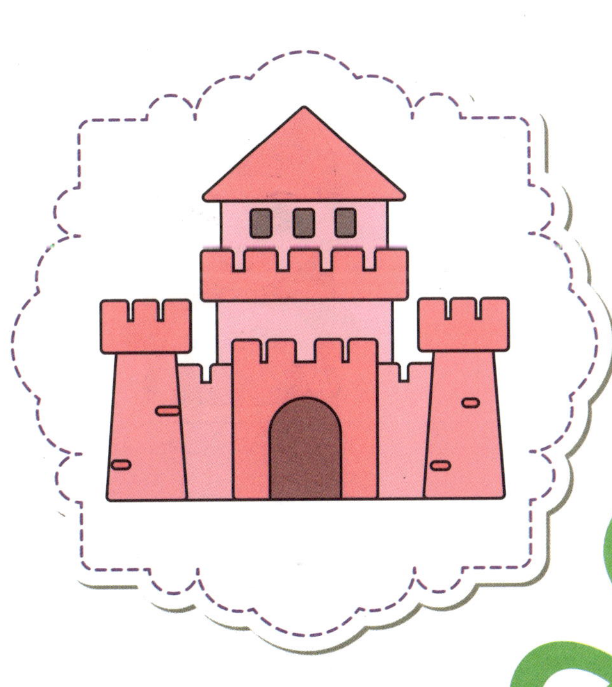

PRINCESS BELLA

This is Princess Bella. Blue is her favourite colour.

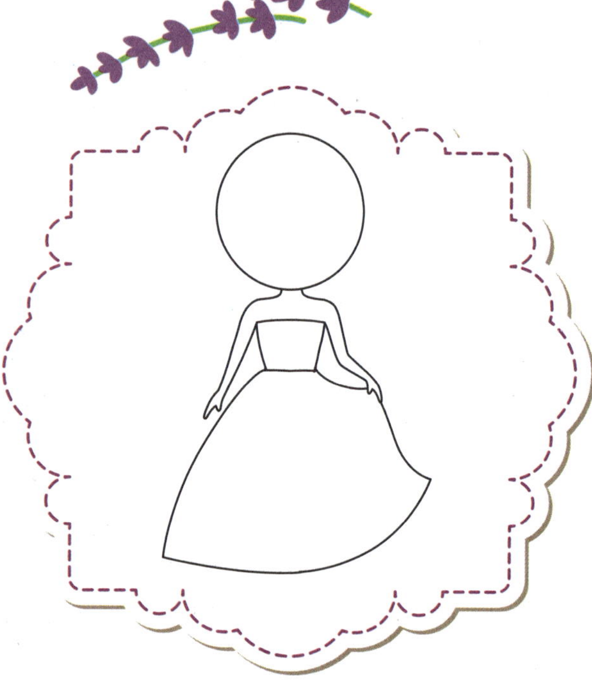

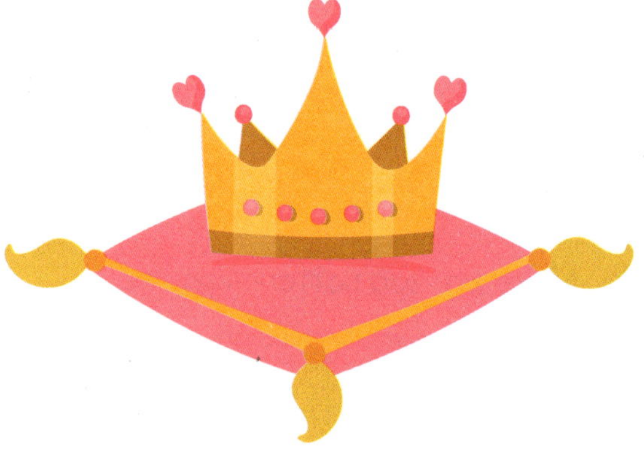

1 Draw a circle for the face. Make arms, an upper body and a gown.

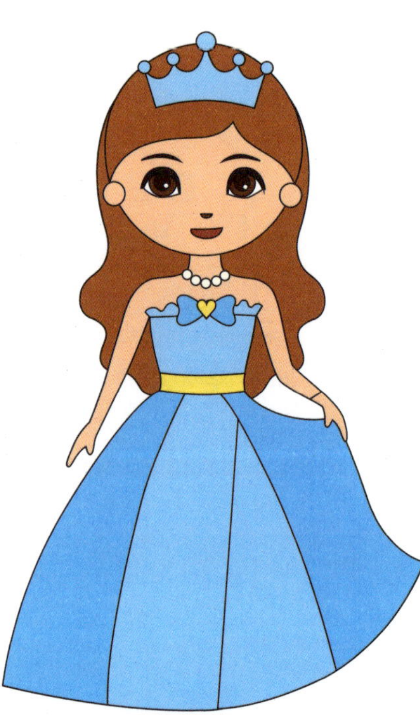

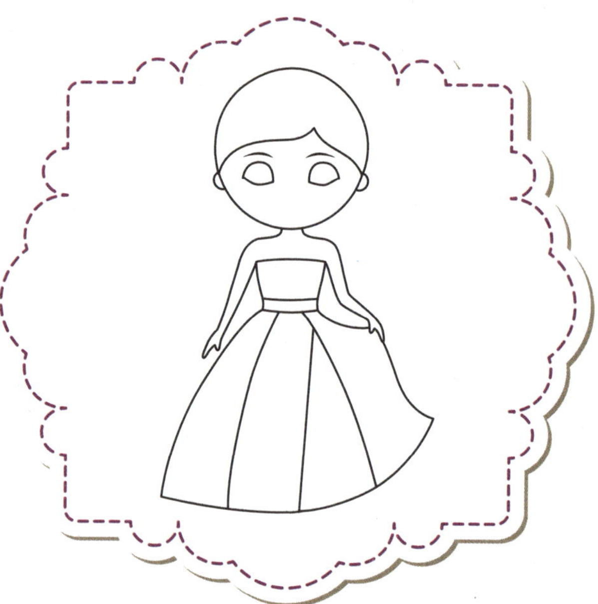

2 Part the head for hair. Draw eyebrows, eyes and lines on the gown.

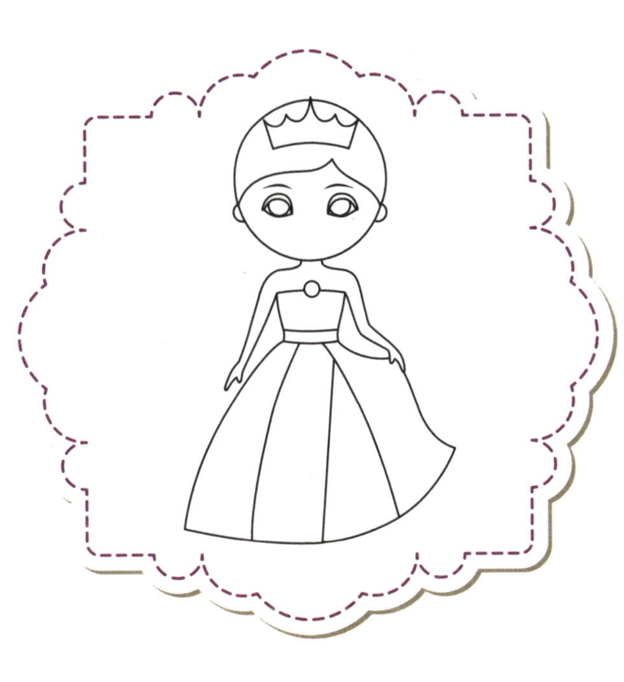

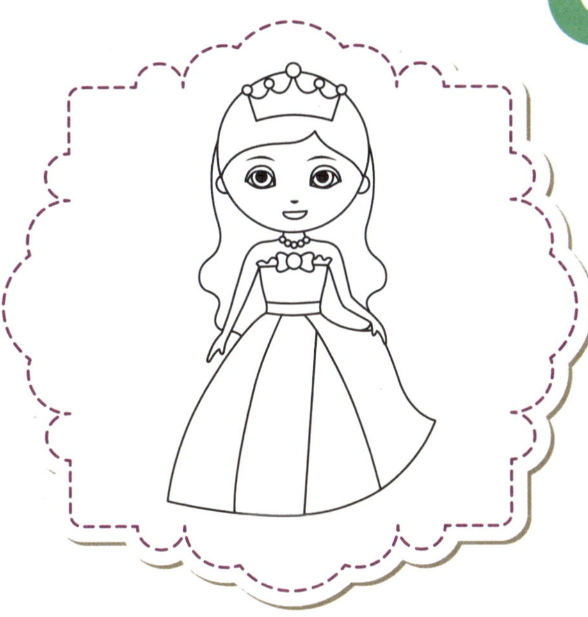

3 Draw a crown and a circle at the centre of the upper part of the gown.

4 Draw a necklace, a design on the upper part of the gown and long hair.

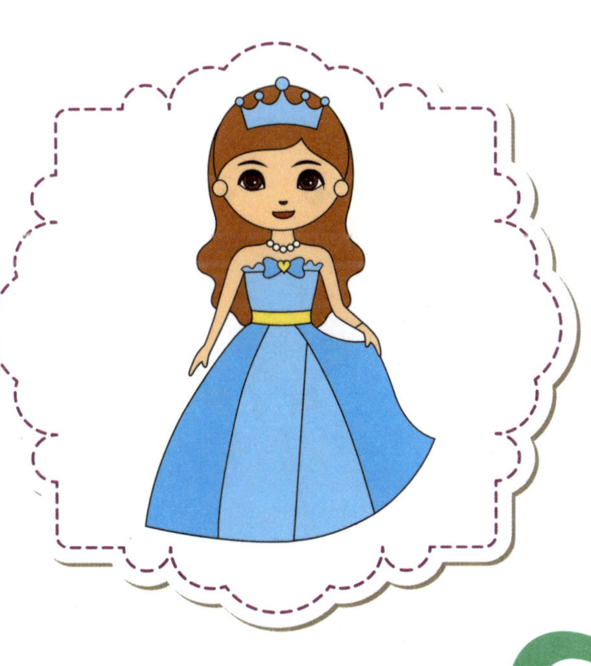

PRINCESS ALICE

This is Princess Alice. She loves her pink gown.

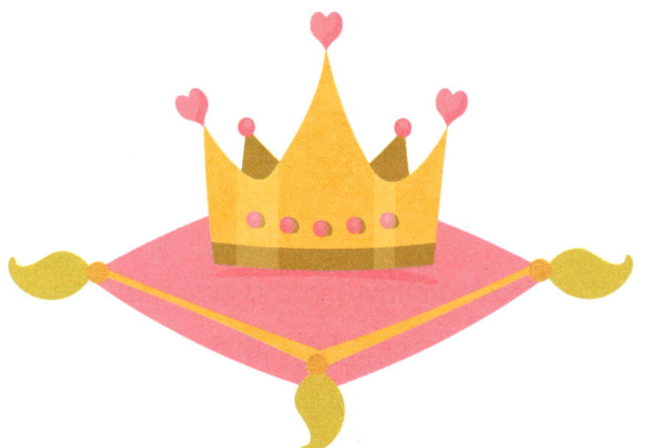

1 Draw a circle for the face. Draw the body, gown and arms.

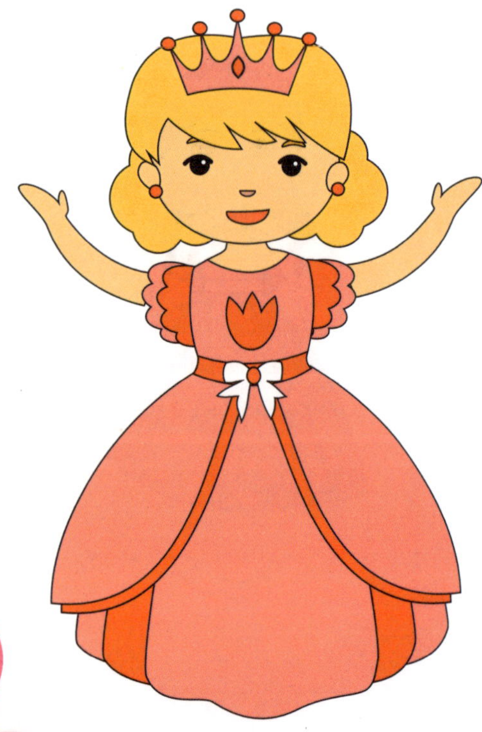

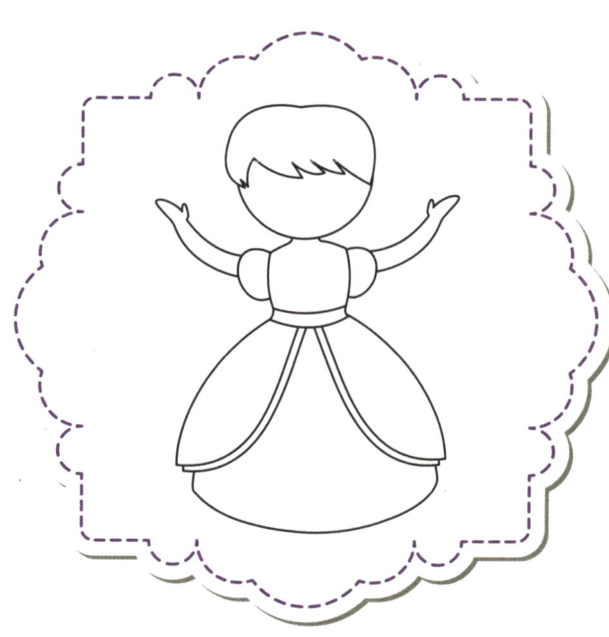

2 Make a partition for the hair on the circle. Draw an outline on the gown.

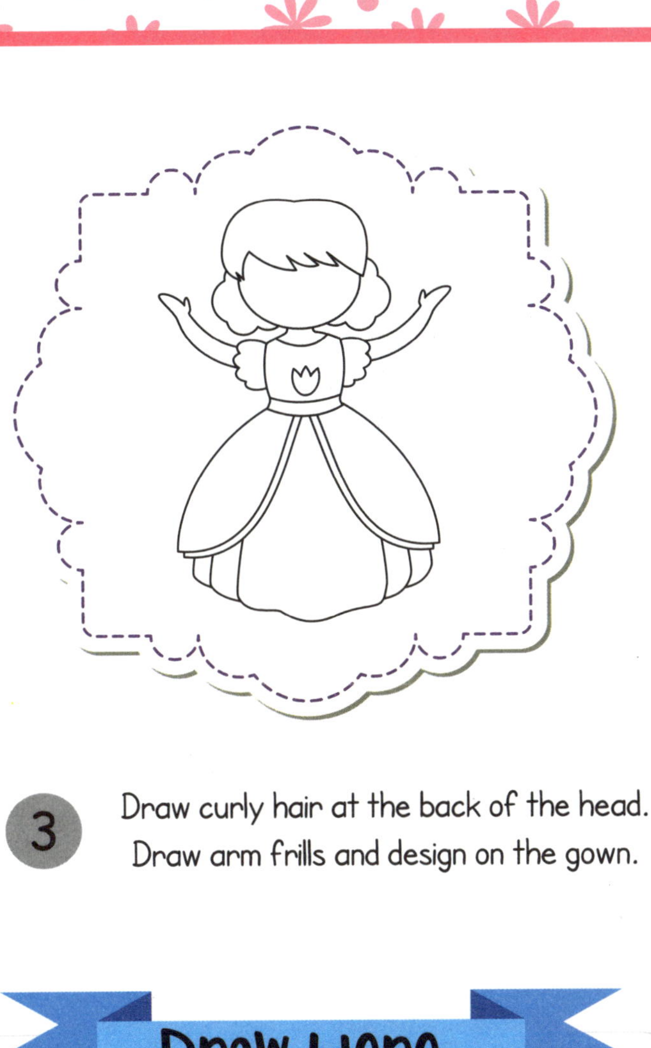

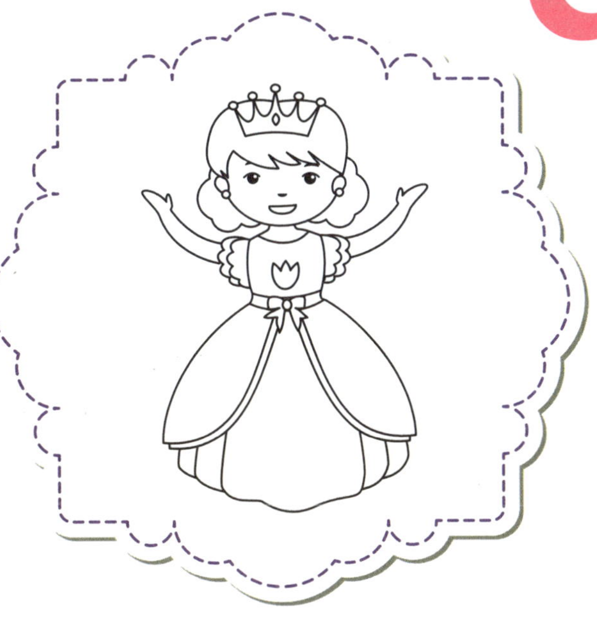

3 Draw curly hair at the back of the head. Draw arm frills and design on the gown.

4 Draw the crown and outline the frills and add a bow on the belt.

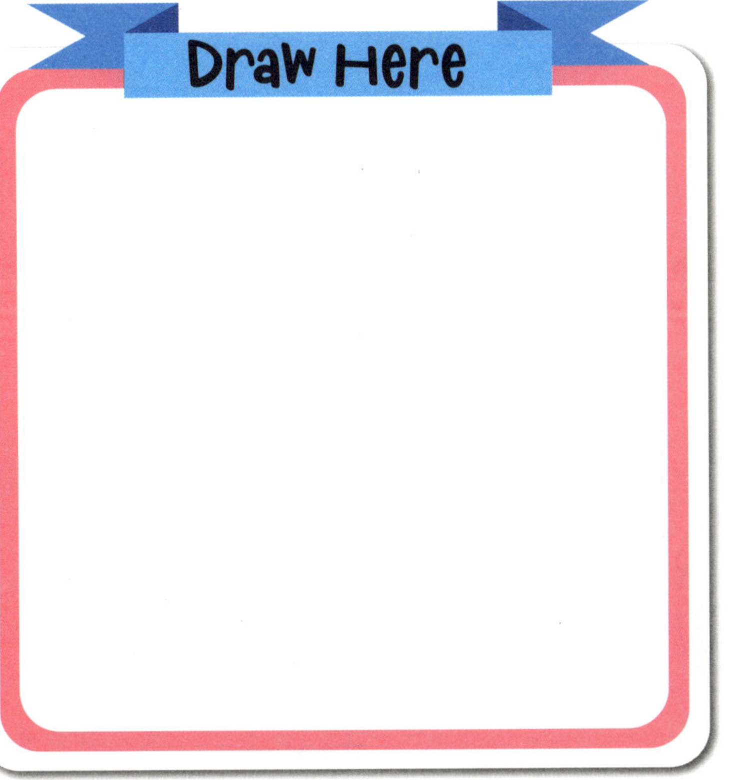

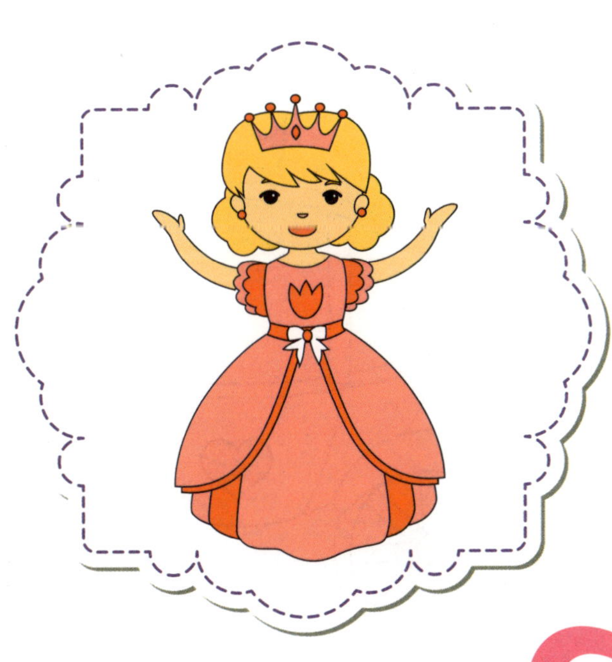

PRINCESS' CHARIOT

This is a princess' chariot. She often travels in it.

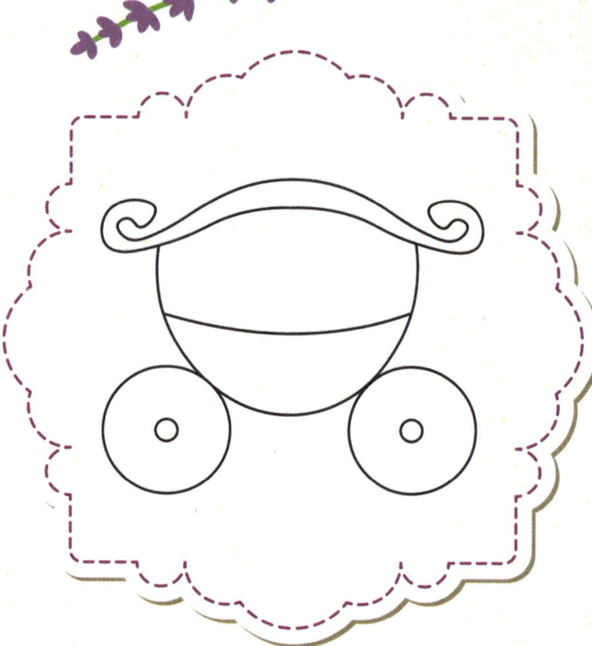

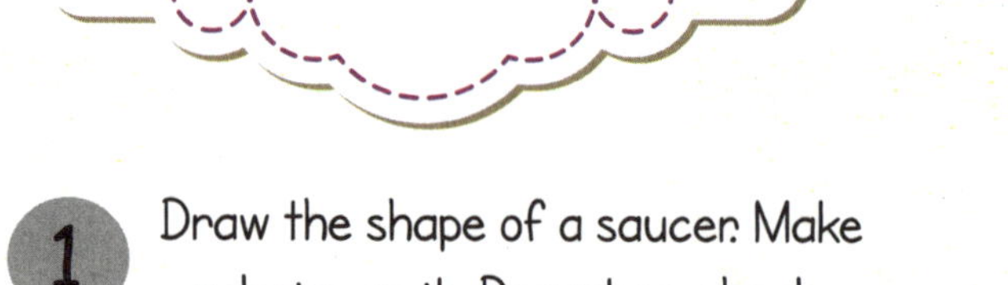

1 Draw the shape of a saucer. Make a design on it. Draw two wheels.

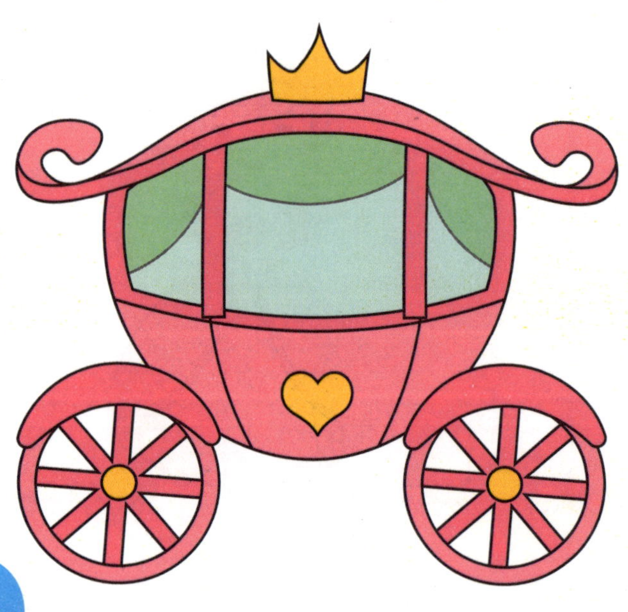

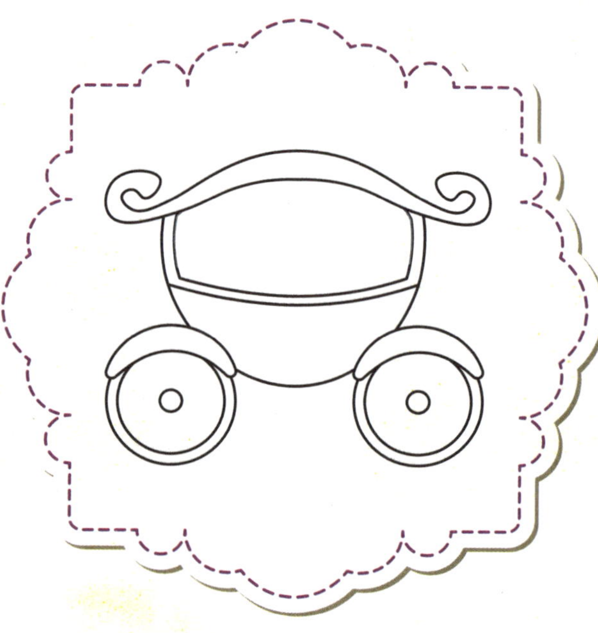

2 Draw the outlines of the chariot. Make mudguards for the wheels.

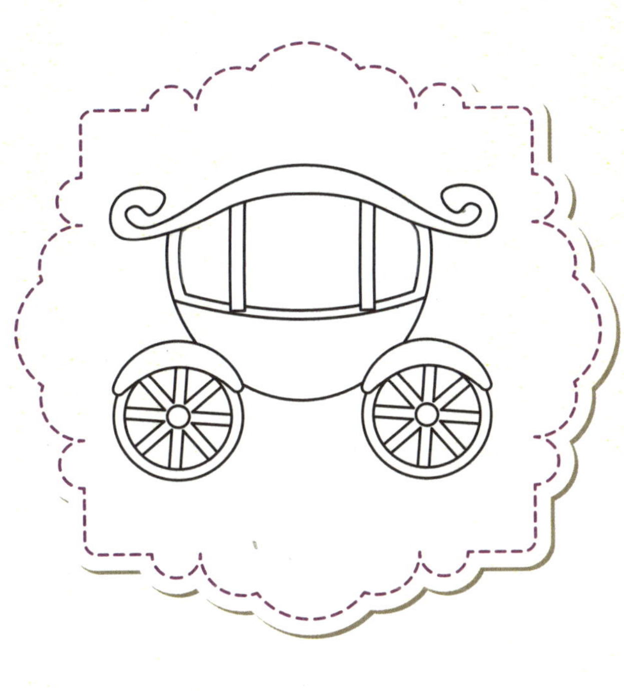

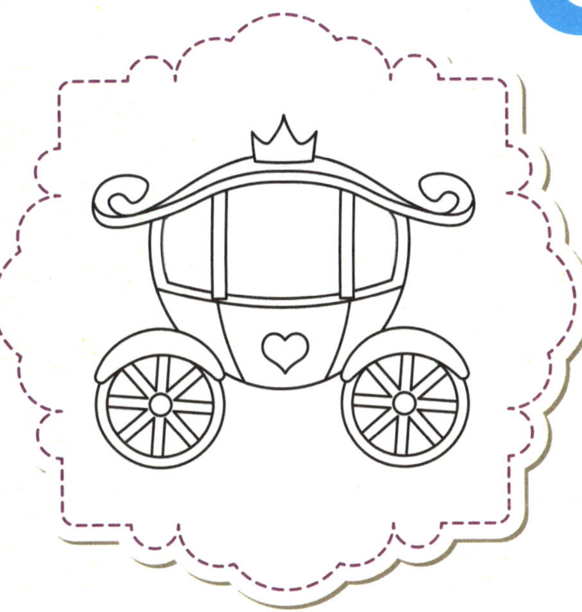

3 Draw spokes on the wheels. Make two bars for the windows.

4 Draw a crown shape at the top of the chariot and a heart shape at the bottom.

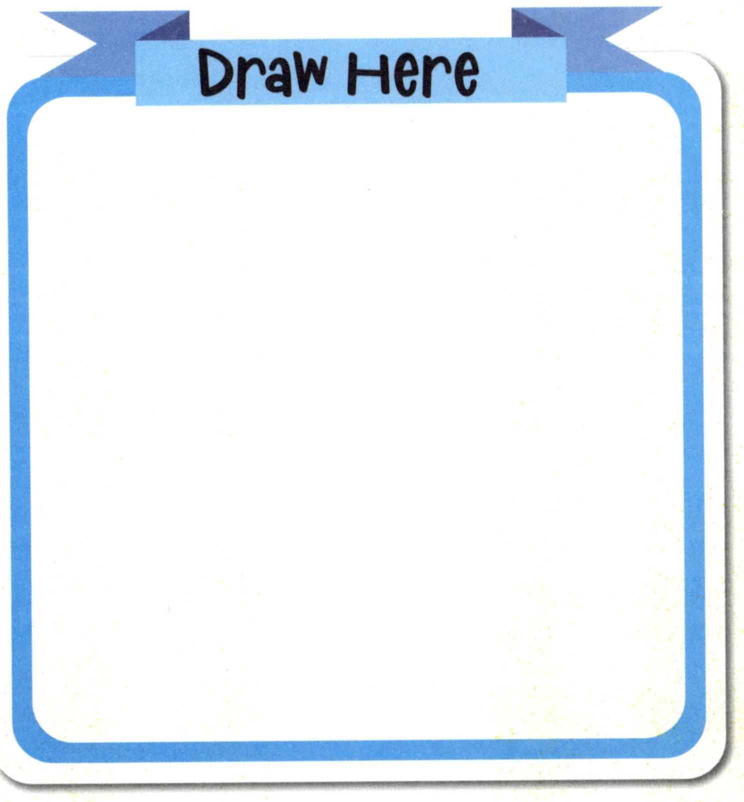

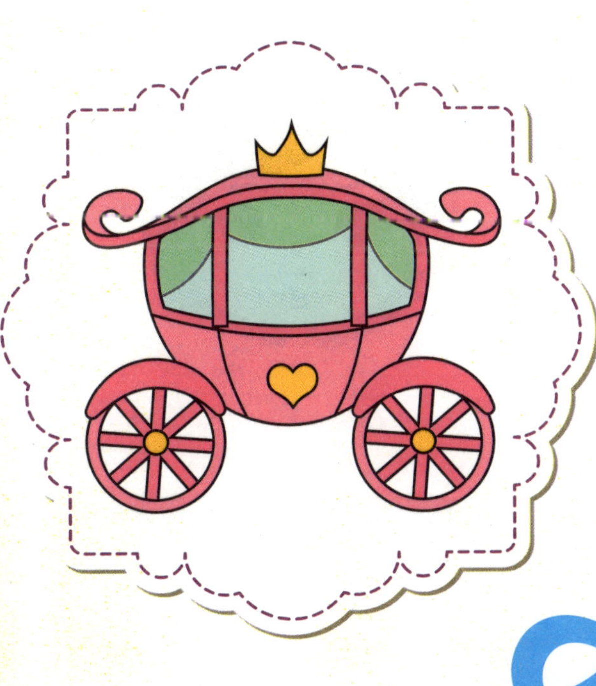

PRINCESS STELLA

This is Princess Stella. She has short hair and likes going on adventures.

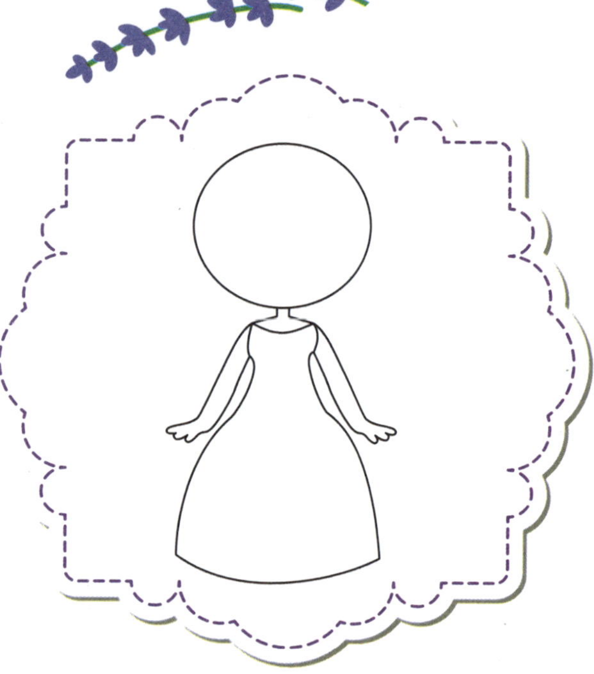

1 Draw a circle for the face. Make arms and the body.

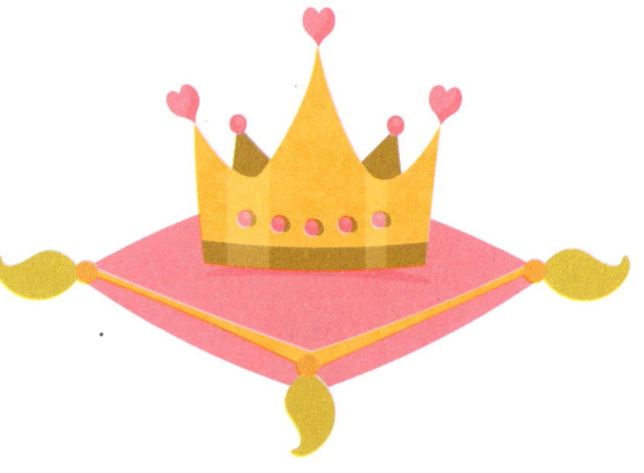

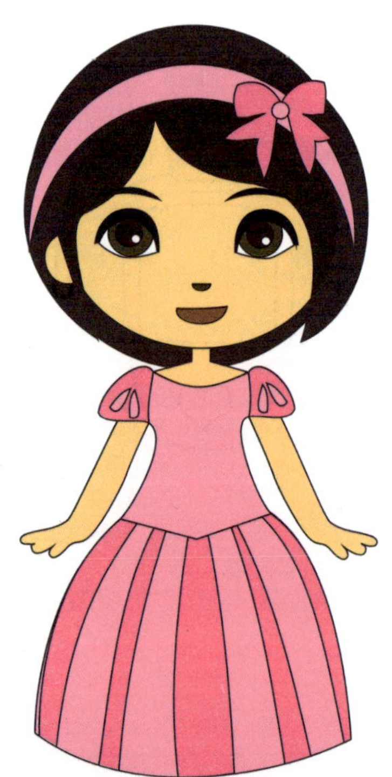

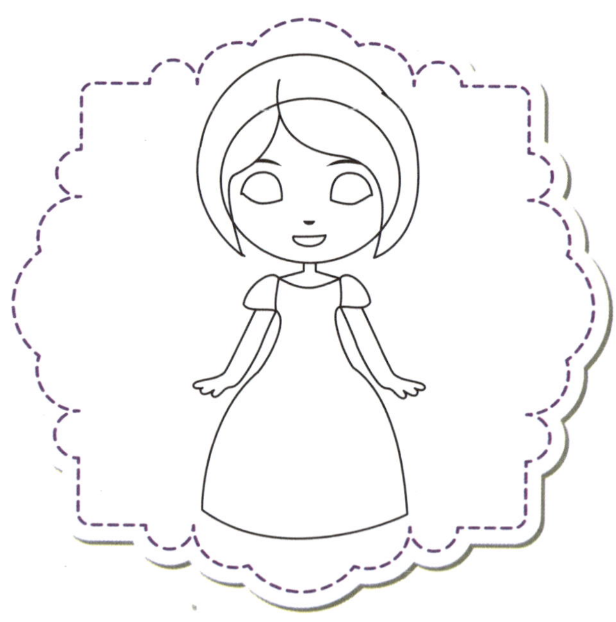

2 Add hair, eyes, nose and mouth. Draw the gown's sleeves.

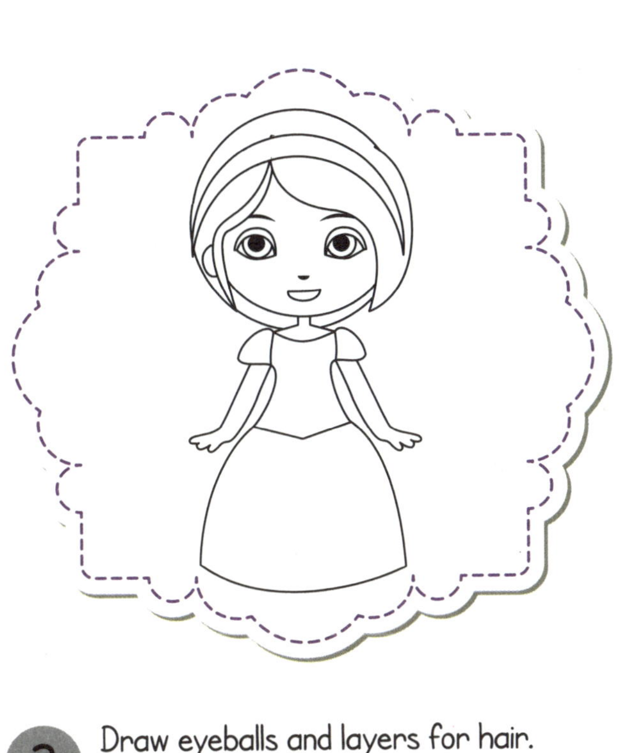

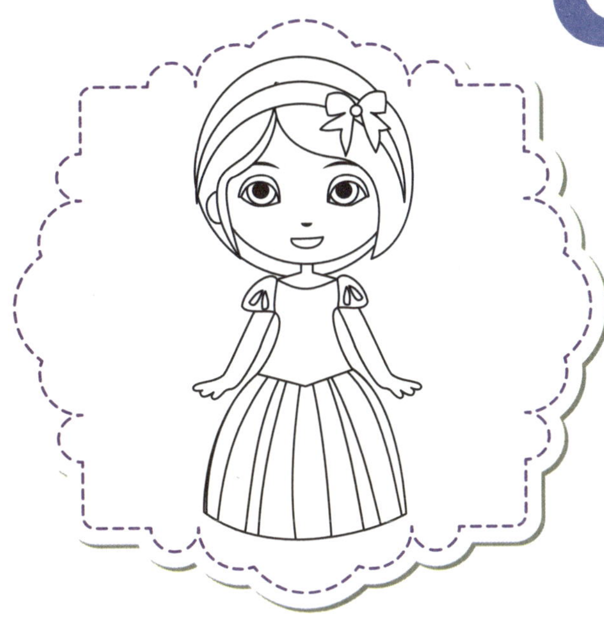

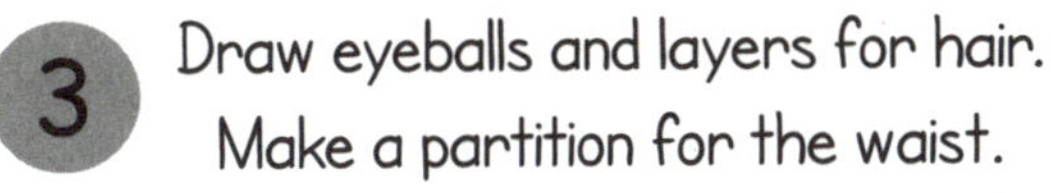

3 Draw eyeballs and layers for hair. Make a partition for the waist.

4 Draw a bow on the head and a design on the sleeves and gown. Colour to complete.

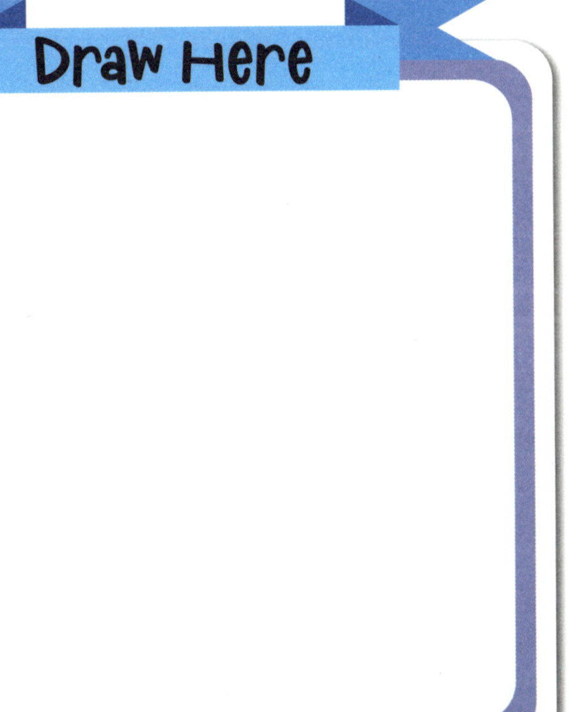

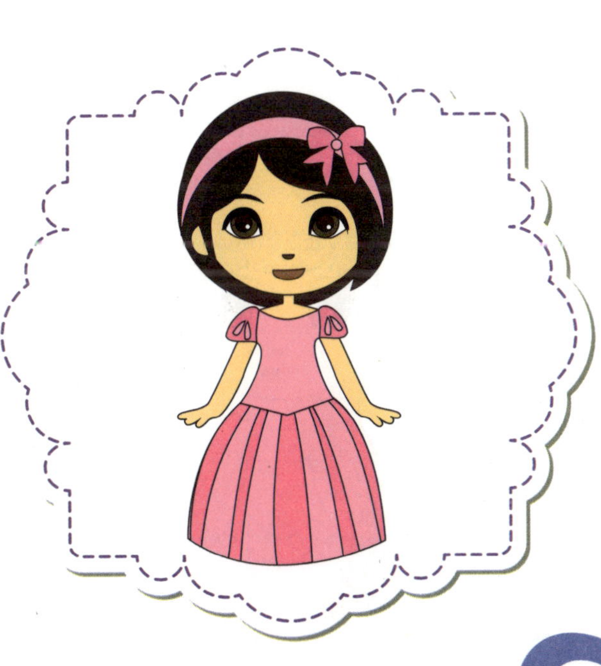

PRINCESS MARIGOLD

This is Princess Marigold. She has long, luscious, golden hair.

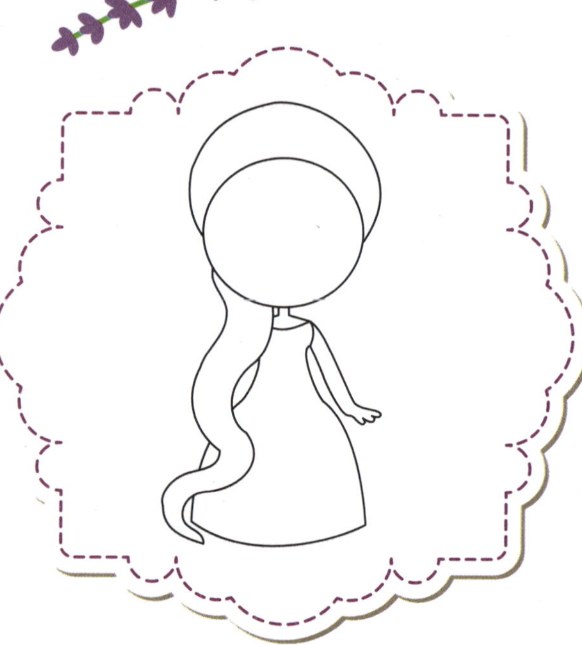

1 Draw a circle for the head and face. Add hair, an upper body and a lower body.

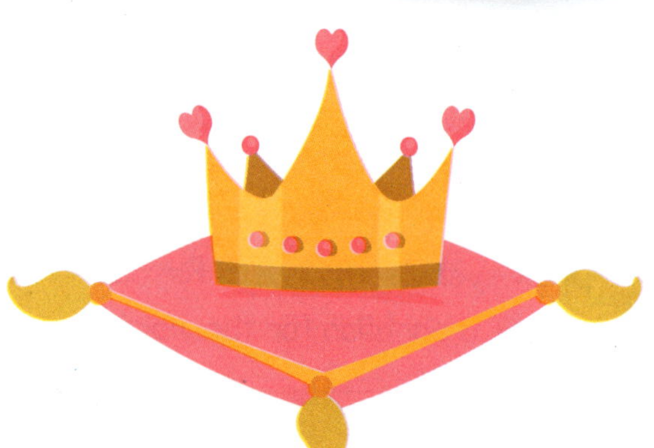

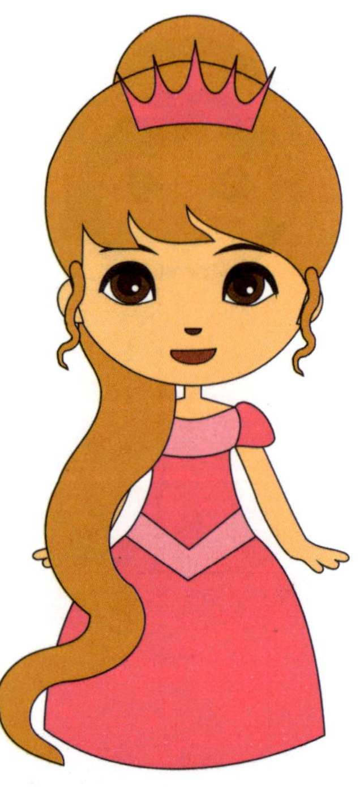

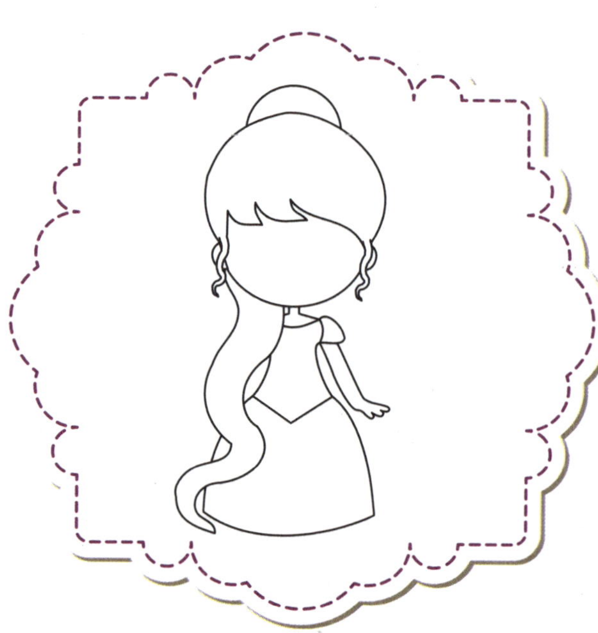

2 Draw a bun and curves for hair. Draw earrings, a sleeve and lines in the middle to make the gown.

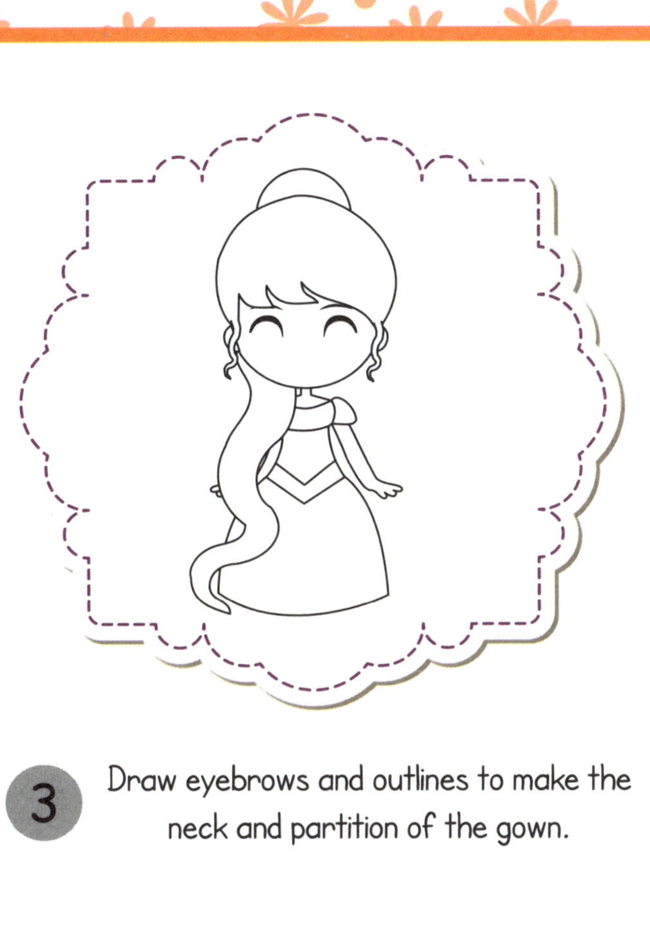

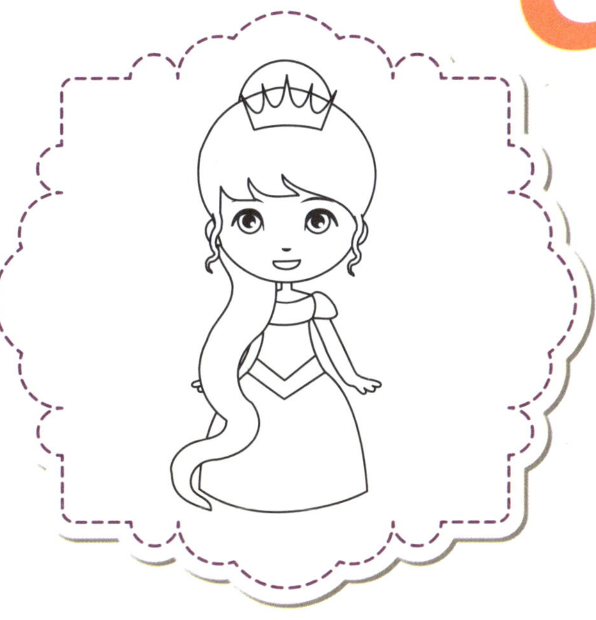

3 Draw eyebrows and outlines to make the neck and partition of the gown.

4 Draw the crown, eyes, nose and mouth. Colour to complete.

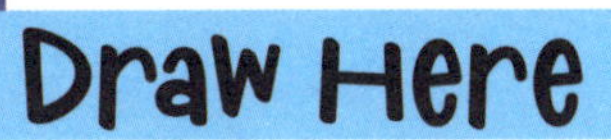

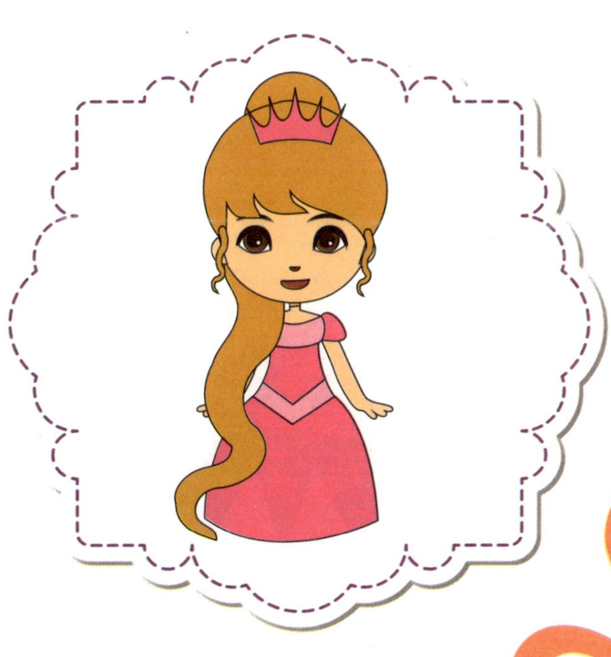

BUTTERFLY

This is a butterfly. It has a thin body and four brightly coloured wings.

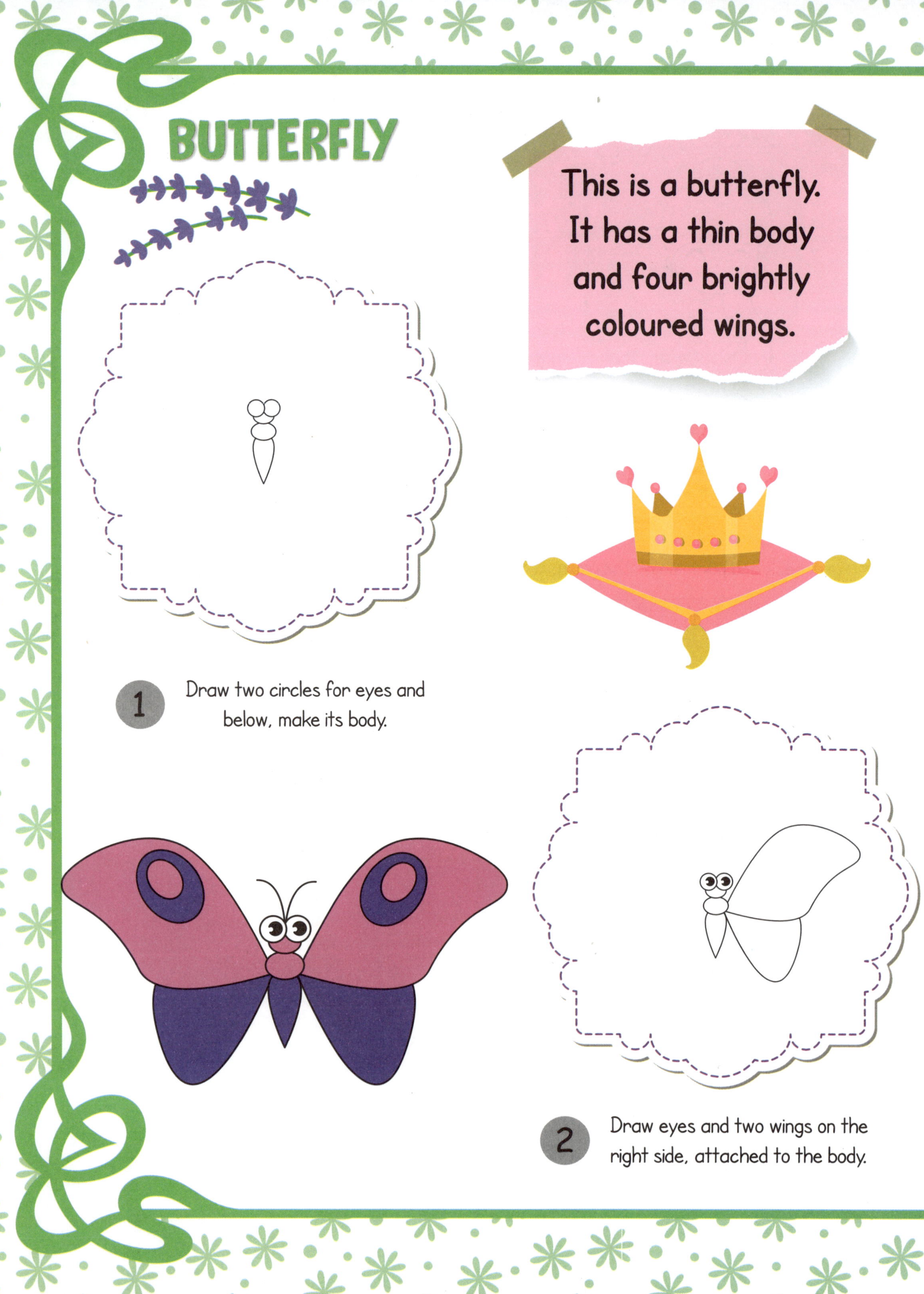

1 Draw two circles for eyes and below, make its body.

2 Draw eyes and two wings on the right side, attached to the body.

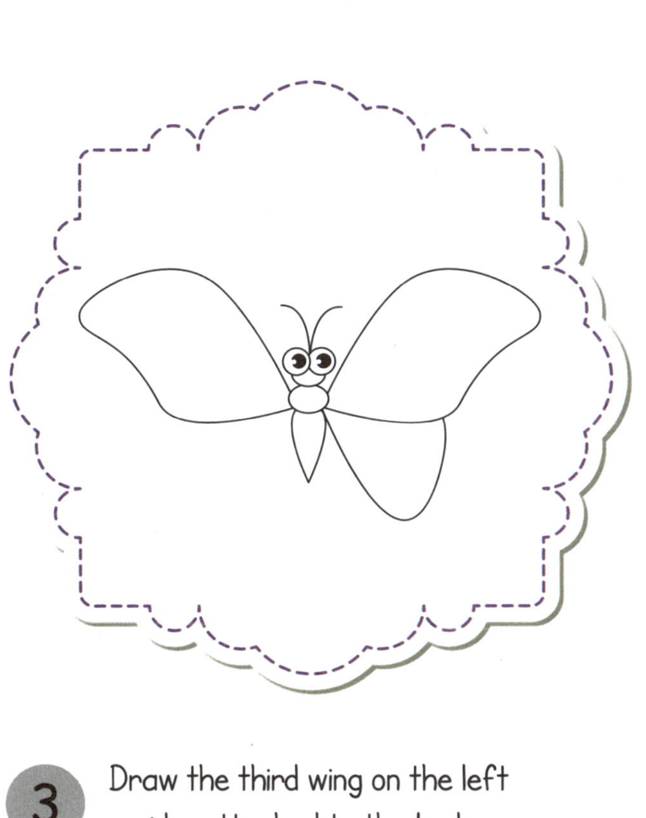

3 Draw the third wing on the left side, attached to the body.

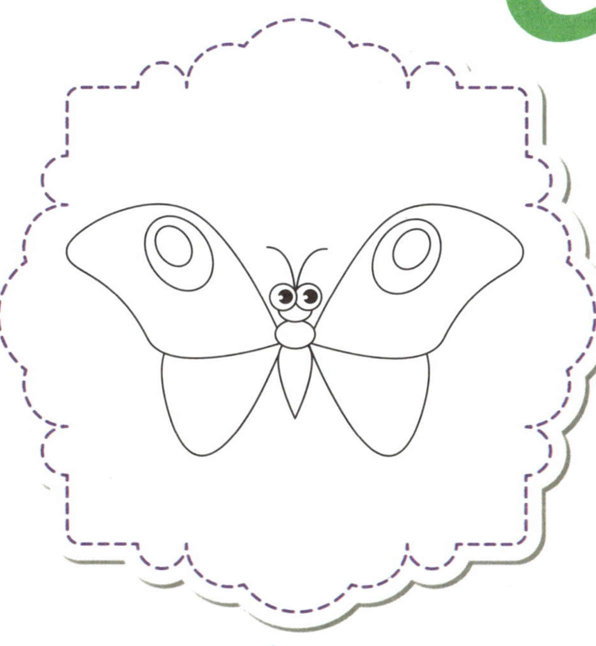

4 Draw the fourth wing and make designs on the upper wings. Colour to complete.

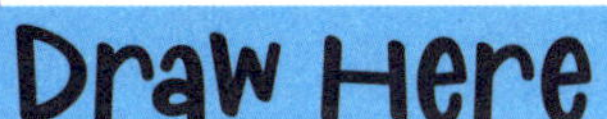

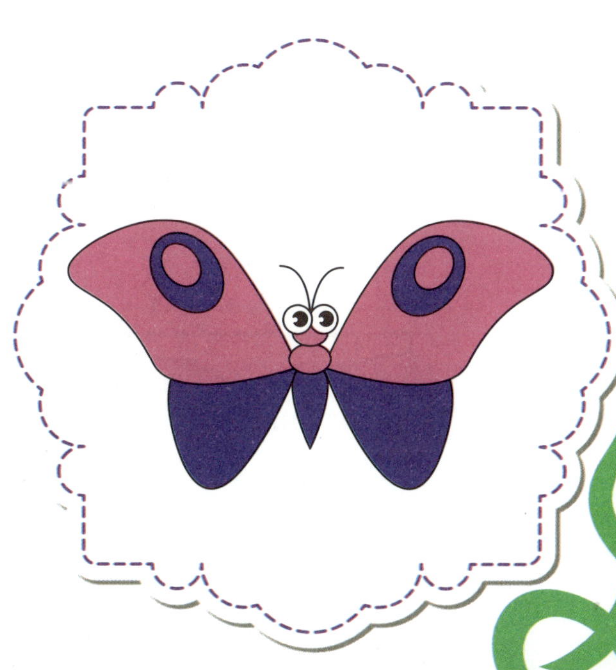

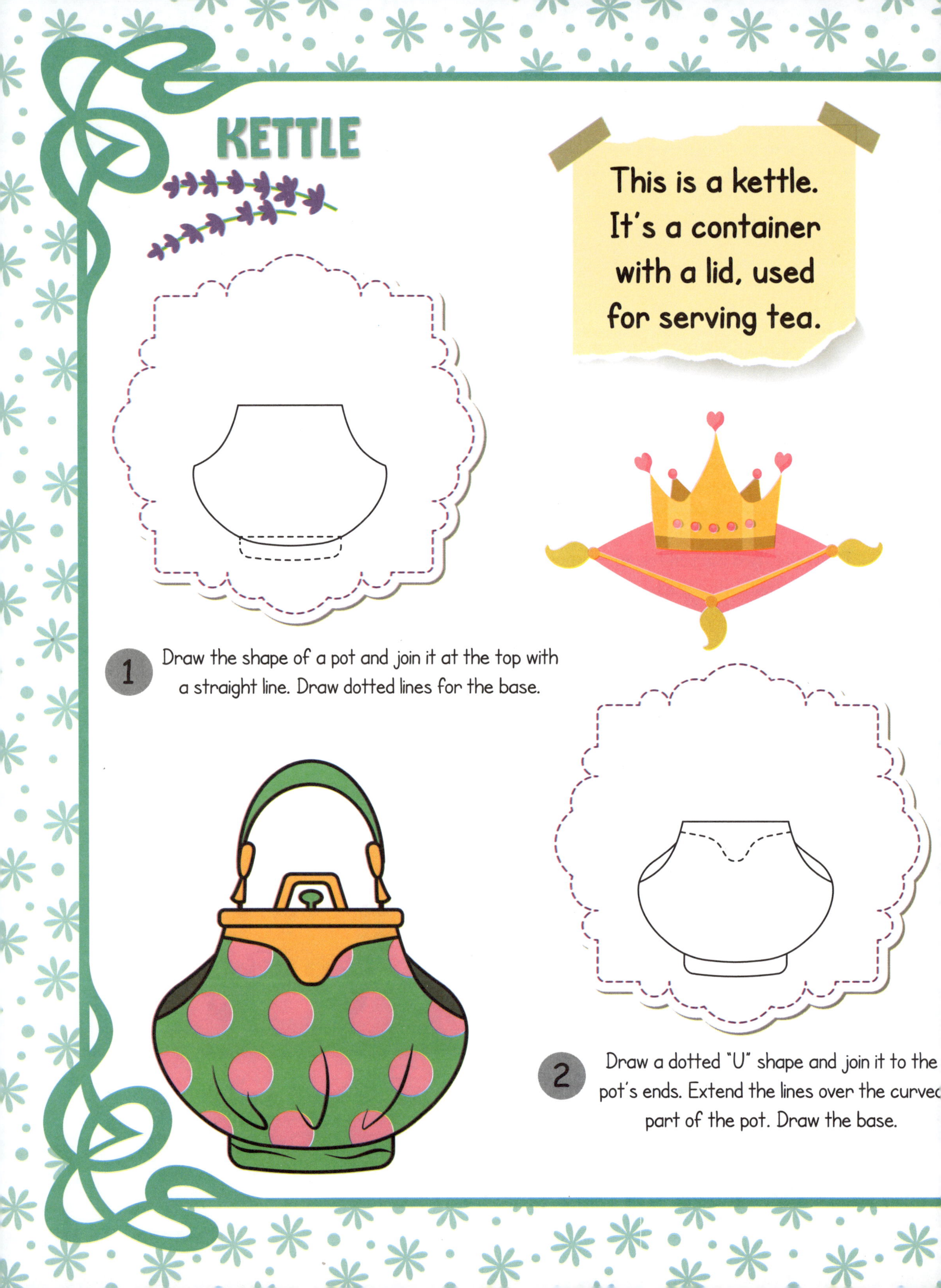

KETTLE

This is a kettle. It's a container with a lid, used for serving tea.

1 Draw the shape of a pot and join it at the top with a straight line. Draw dotted lines for the base.

2 Draw a dotted "U" shape and join it to the pot's ends. Extend the lines over the curved part of the pot. Draw the base.

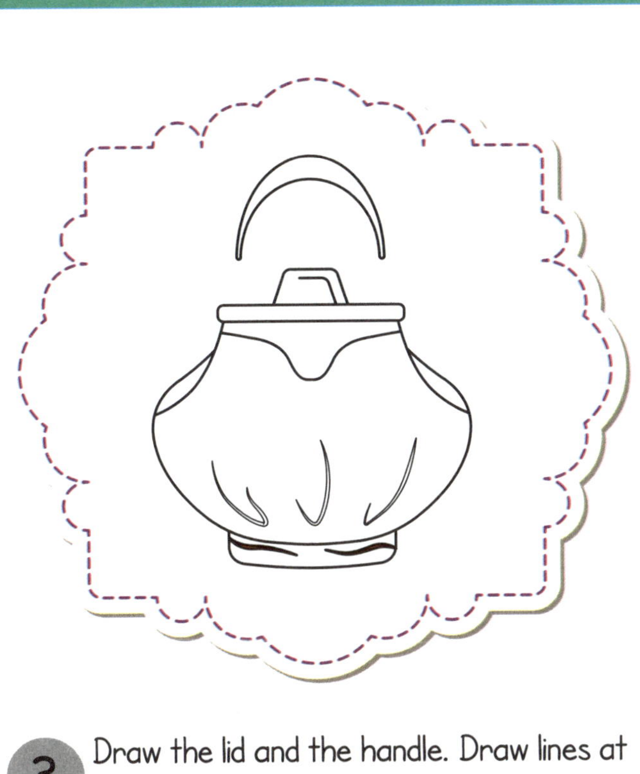

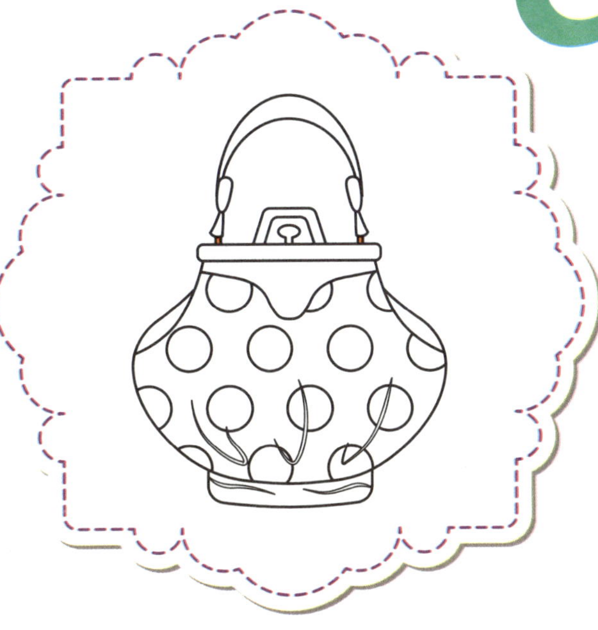

3 Draw the lid and the handle. Draw lines at the base of the pot and inside.

4 Attach the handle to the pot. Draw an outline on the lid and designs on the pot. Colour to complete.

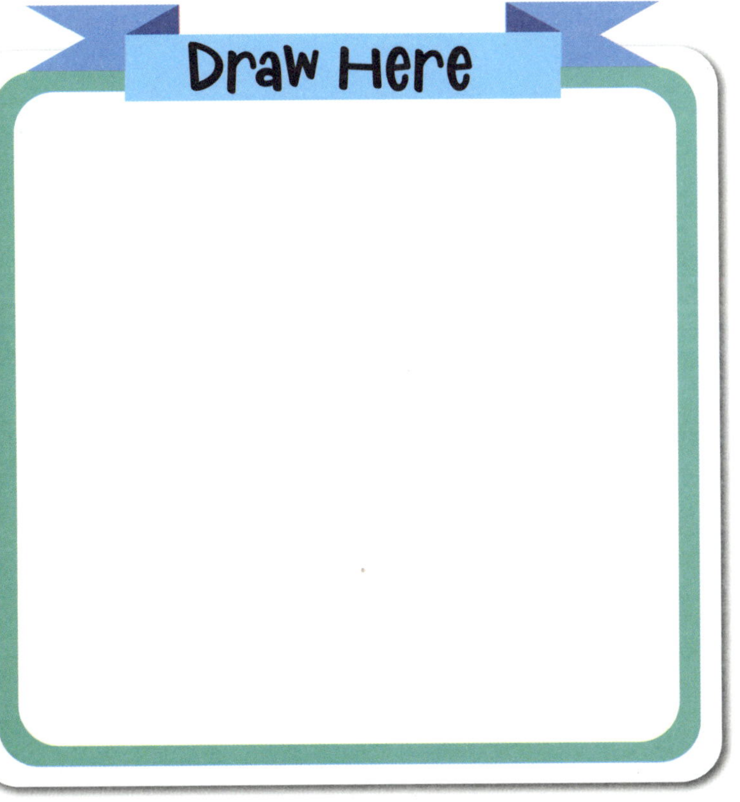

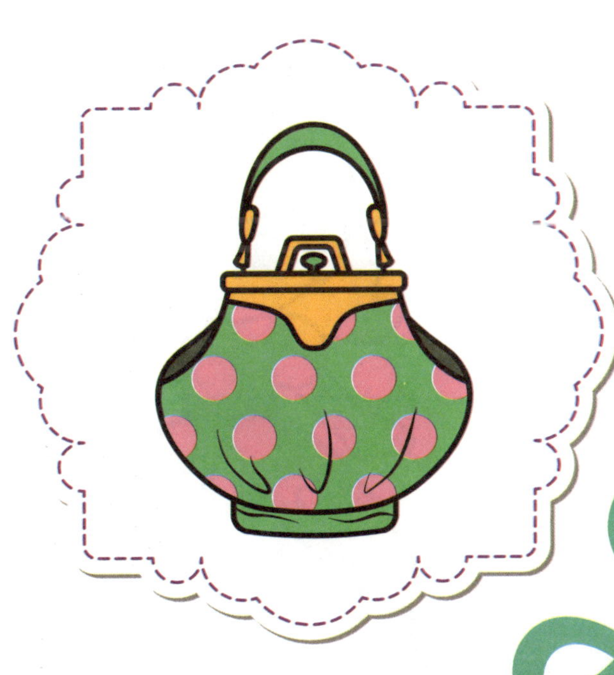

PRINCESS IVY

This is Princess Ivy. She loves flowers.

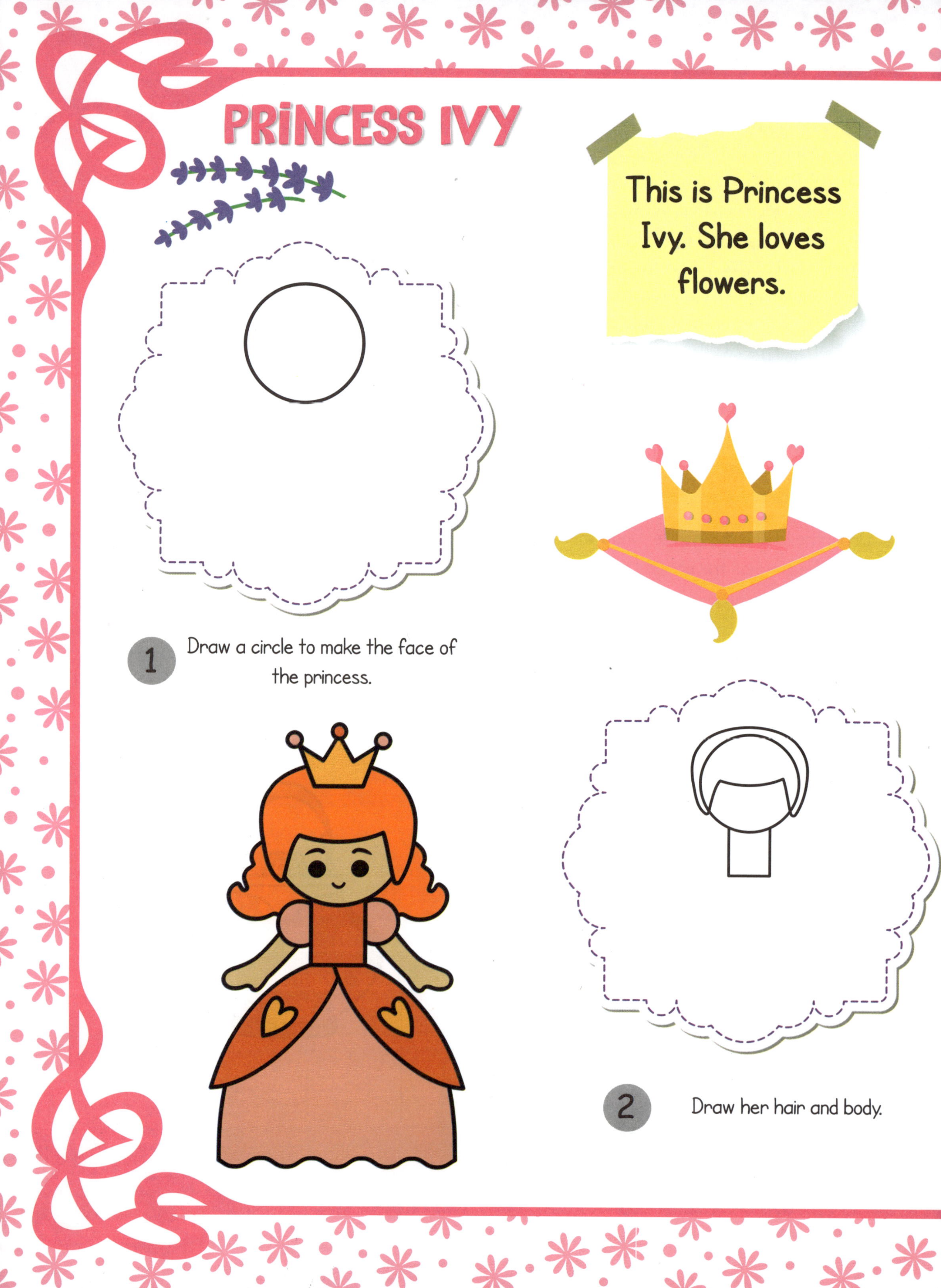

1 Draw a circle to make the face of the princess.

2 Draw her hair and body.

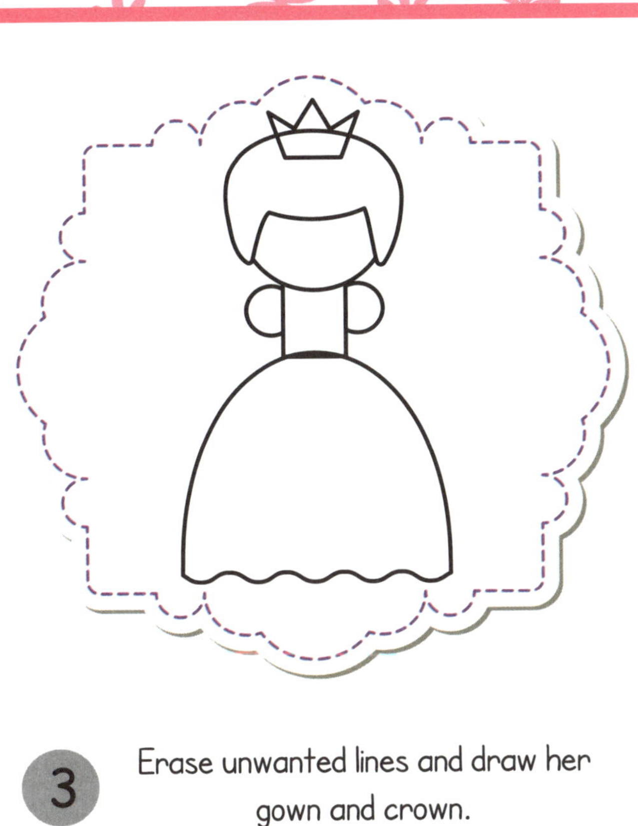

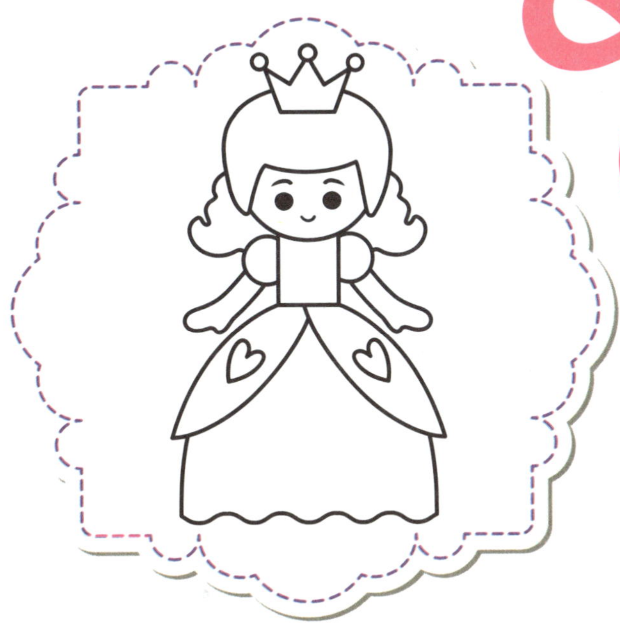

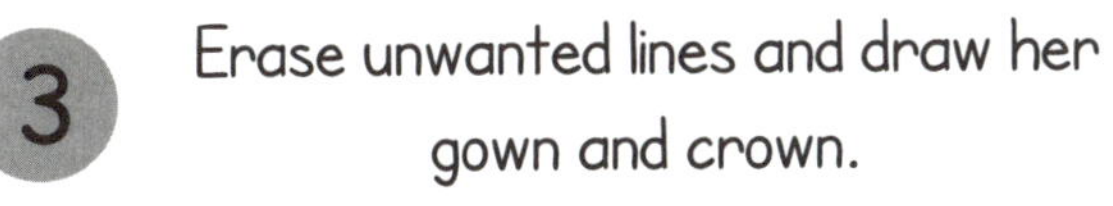

3 Erase unwanted lines and draw her gown and crown.

4 Draw details of her gown. Draw her eyes, hands, hair and colour her beautifully.

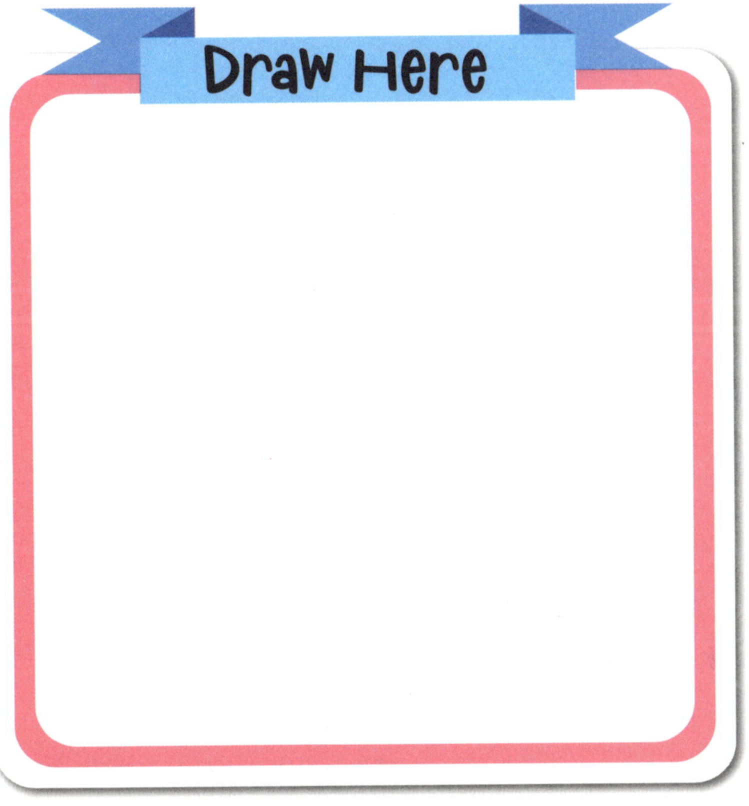

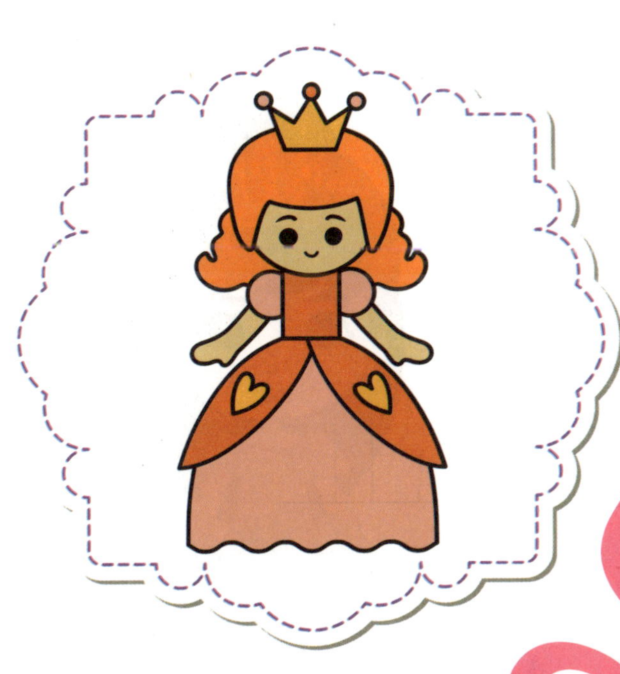

PRINCESS MAPLE

This is Princess Maple. Her favourite colour is purple.

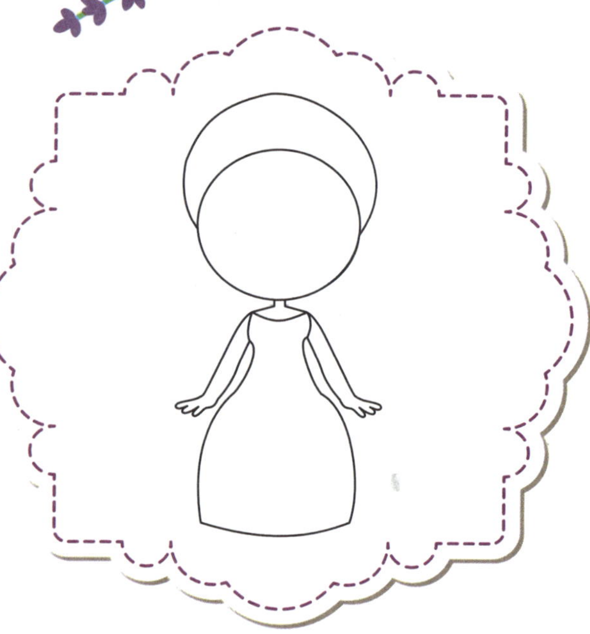

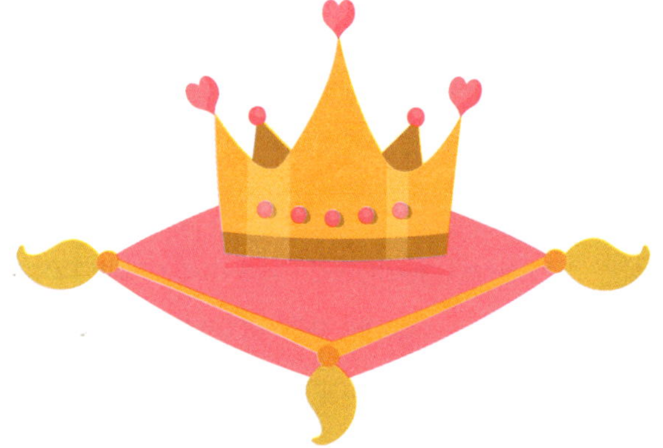

1 Draw a circle for the head. Outline it for hair. Draw the body and arms.

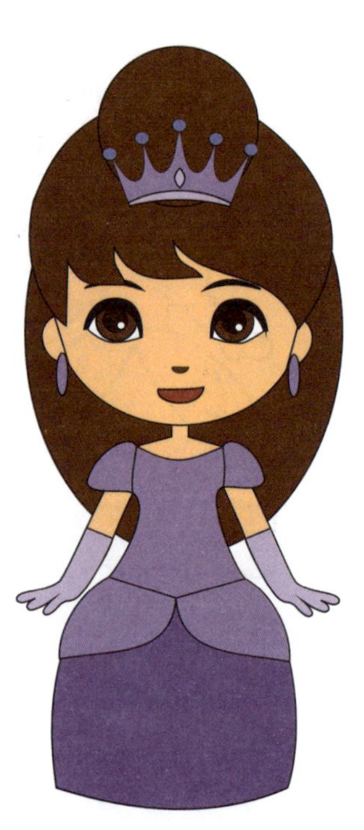

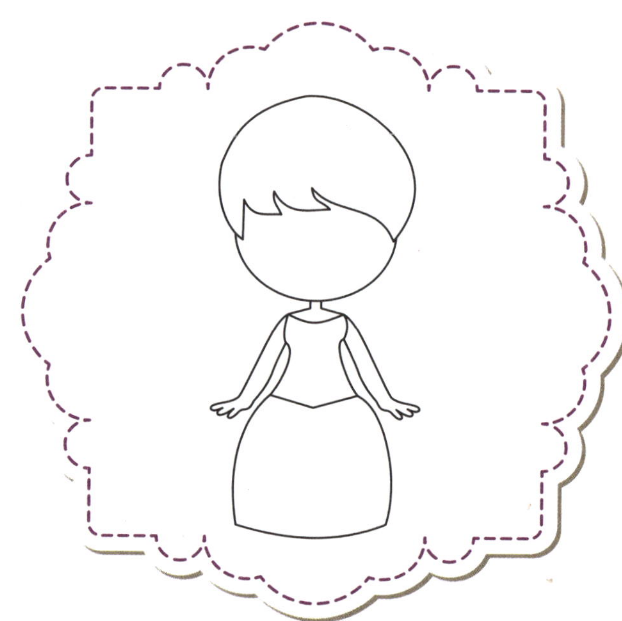

2 Erase unwanted lines. Make curves for the hairstyle. Make a partition in the middle of the gown.

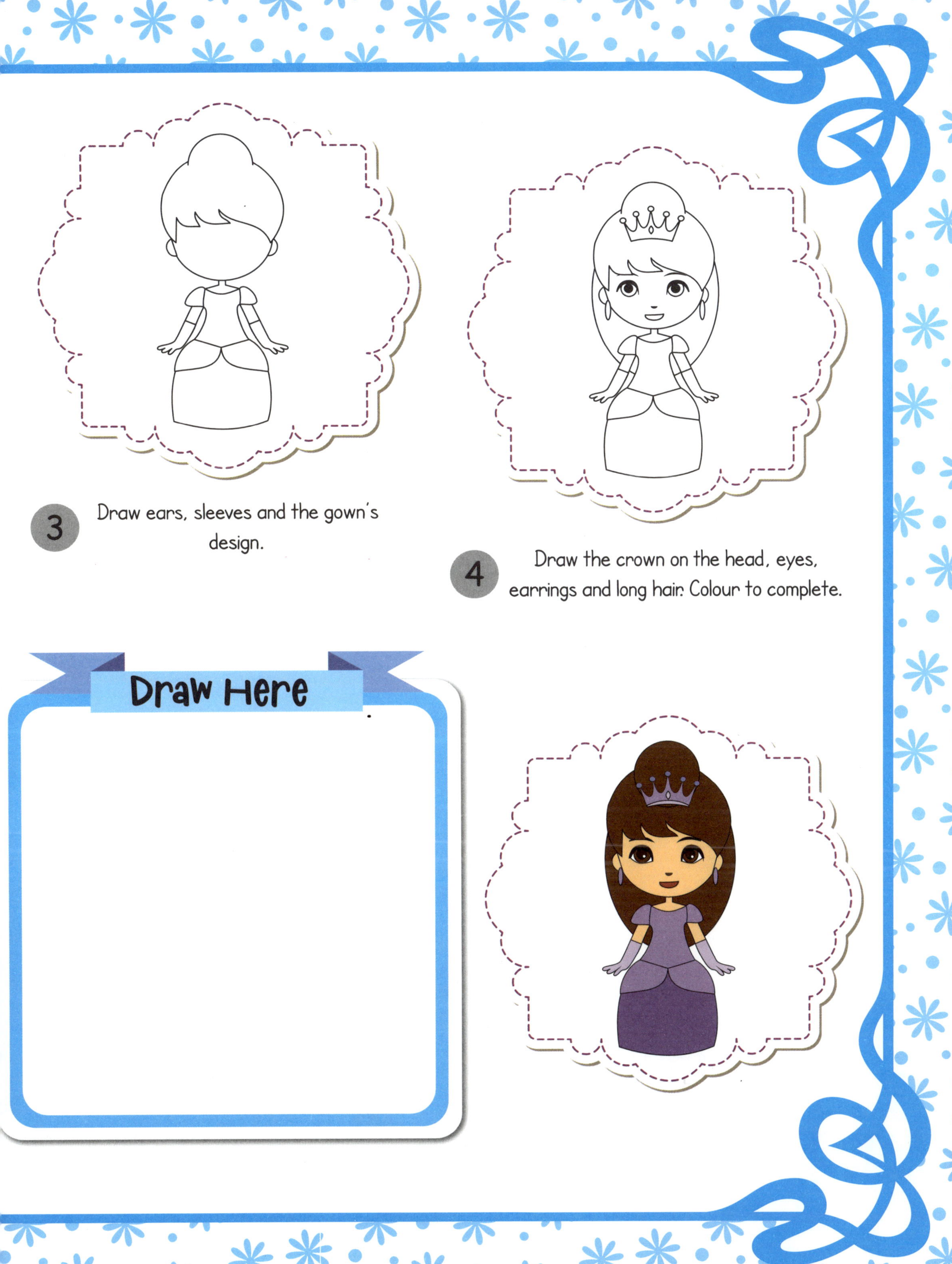
3
Draw ears, sleeves and the gown's design.
4
Draw the crown on the head, eyes, earrings and long hair. Colour to complete.
Draw Here

SANDAL

This is a sandal. A princess wears it on her feet with her pretty gown.

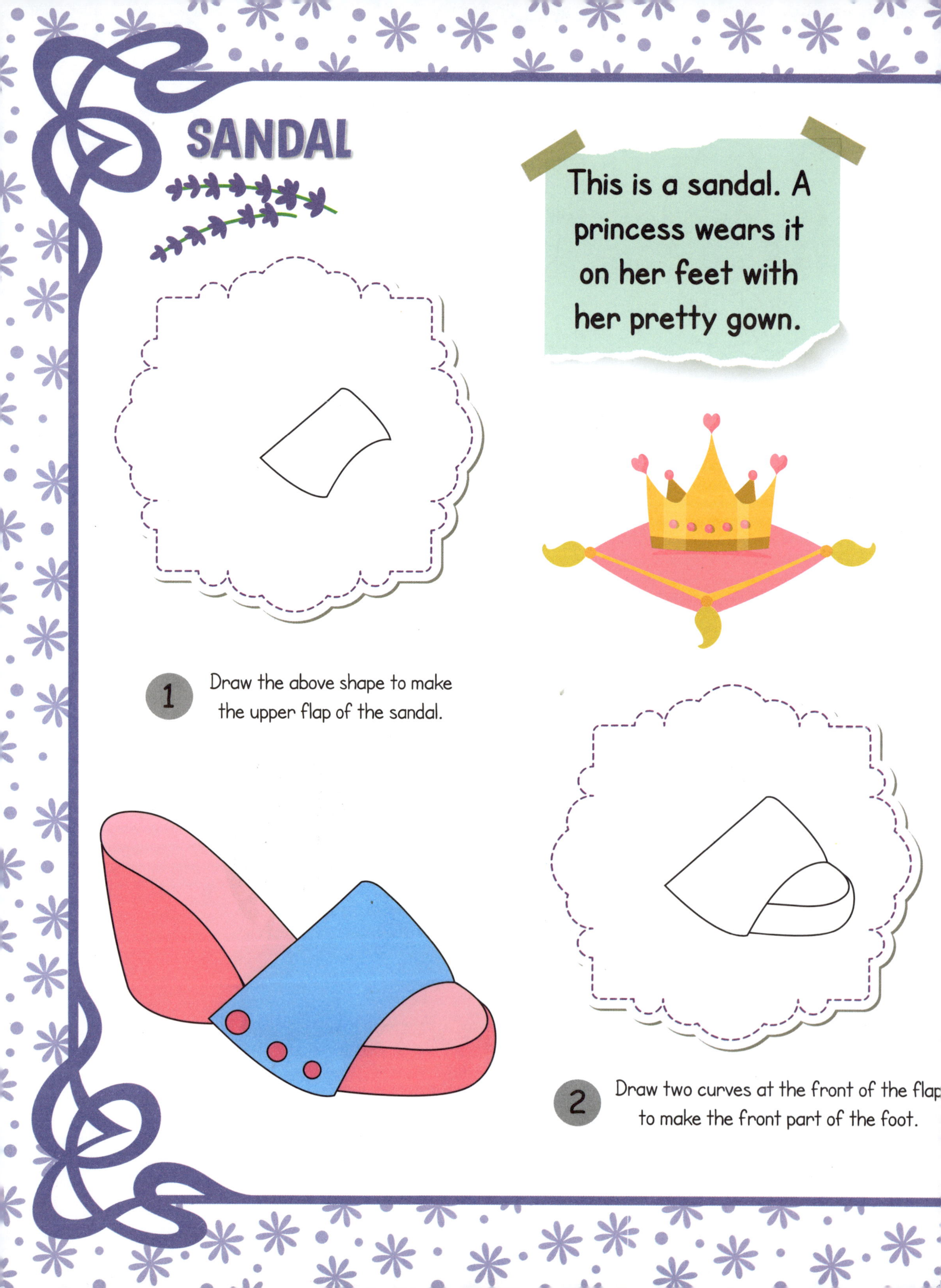

1 Draw the above shape to make the upper flap of the sandal.

2 Draw two curves at the front of the flap to make the front part of the foot.

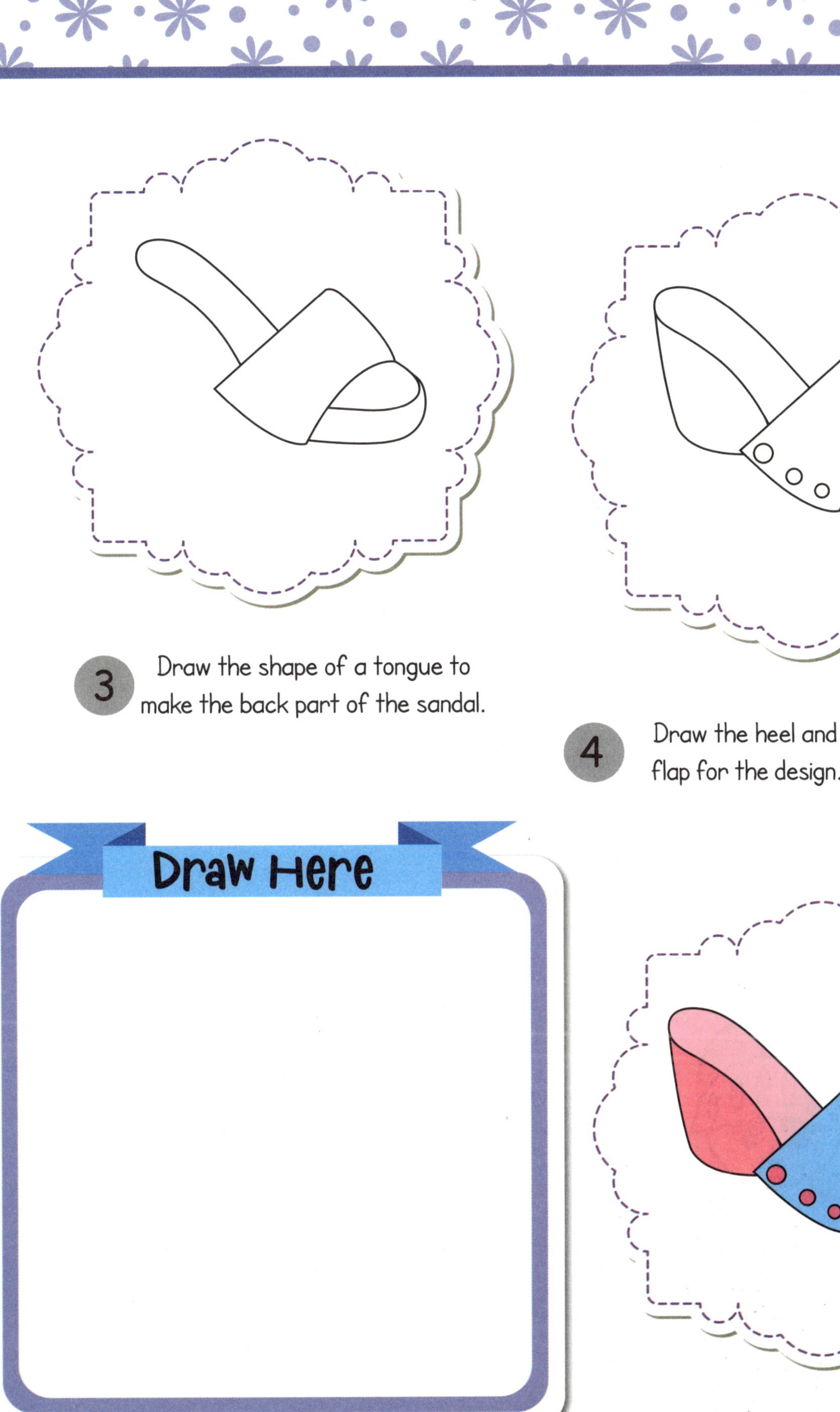

3 Draw the shape of a tongue to make the back part of the sandal.

4 Draw the heel and three circles on the flap for the design. Colour to complete.

Draw Here

KNiGHT

A knight is a strong and loyal soldier.

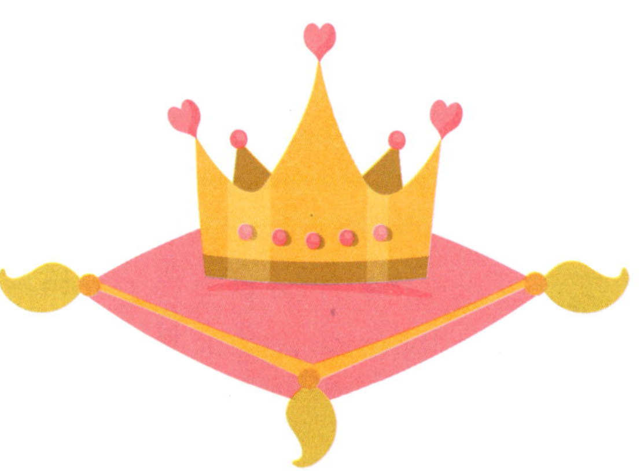

1 Draw a circle for the face and an oval for the body of the knight.

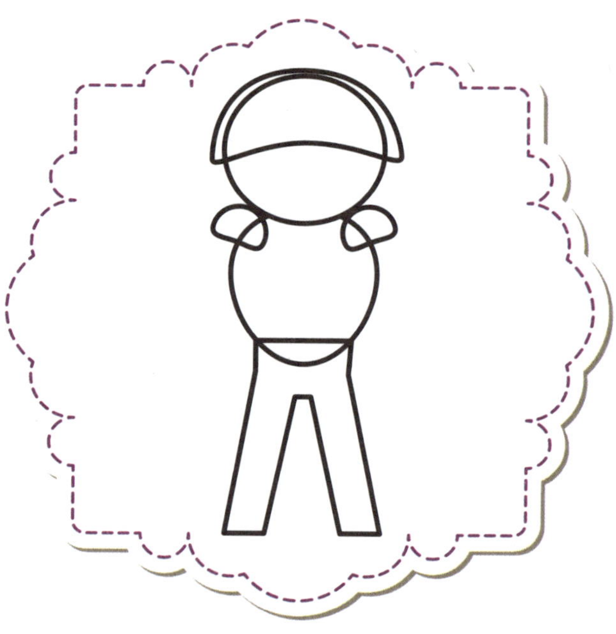

2 Draw his armour, legs and helmet.

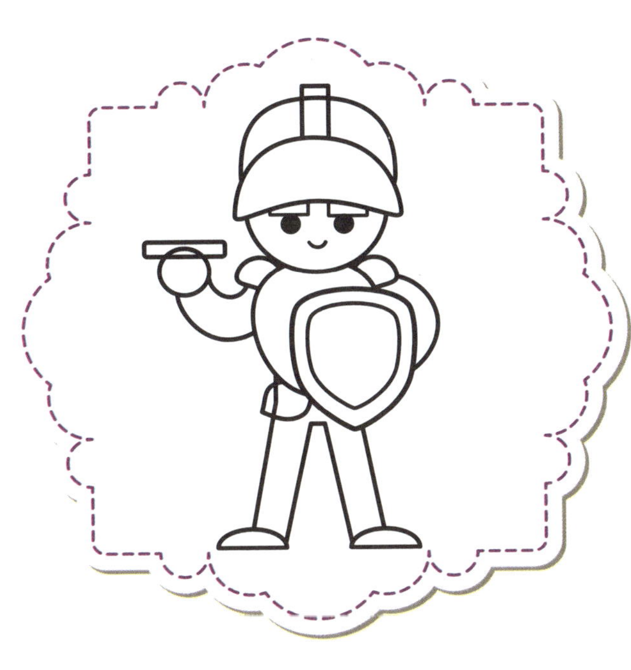

3 Draw his eyes, shield and arm. Draw details on his head as shown.

4 Draw details on his armour, shield and helmet. Draw a sword to complete the knight and colour him.

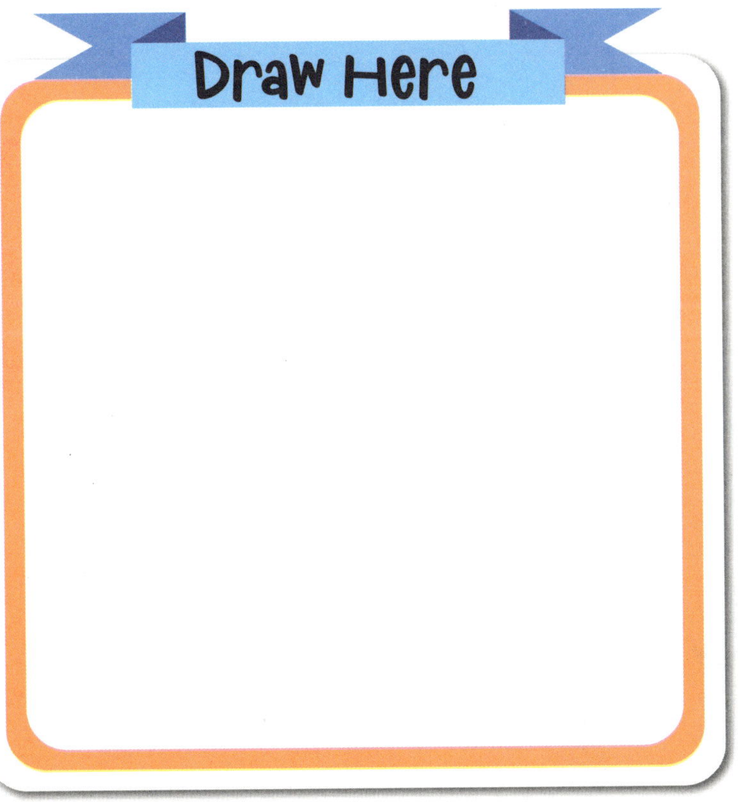

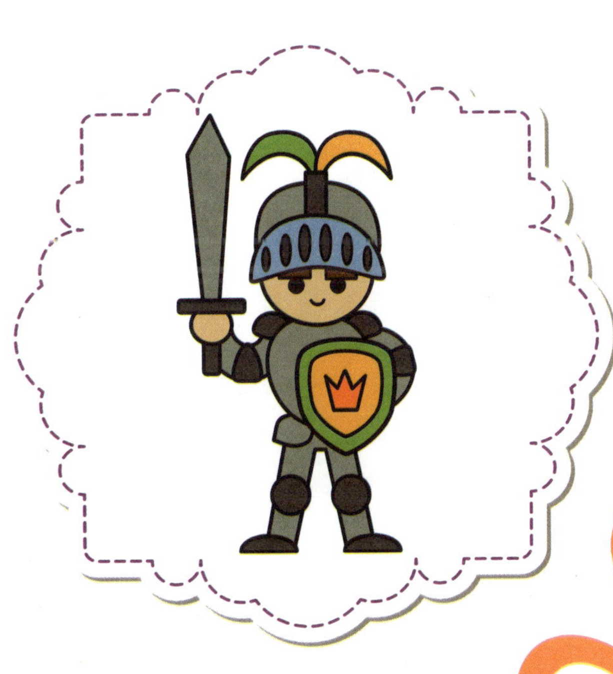

UNICORN

This is a unicorn. It has a horn growing out of its forehead.

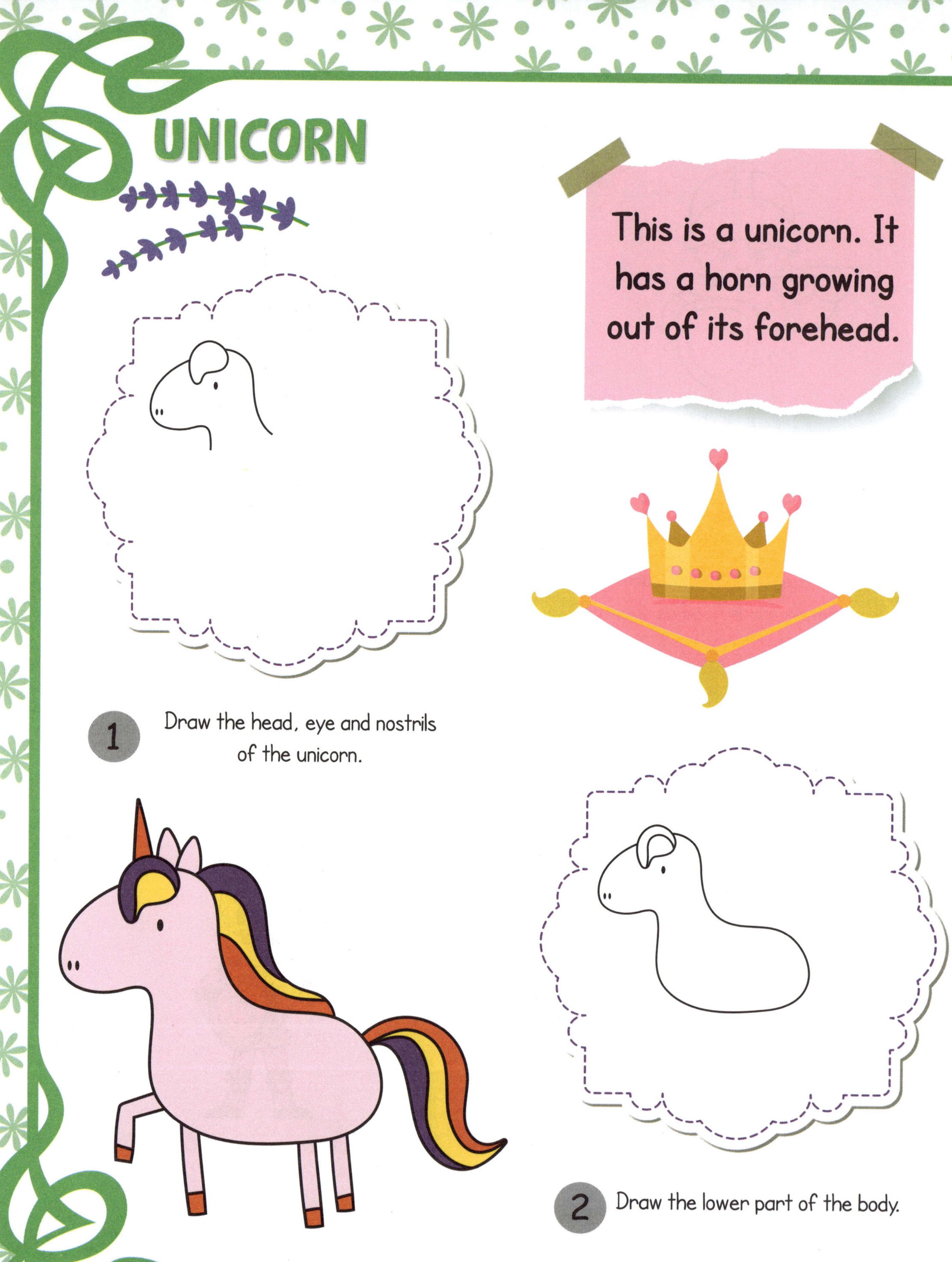

1 Draw the head, eye and nostrils of the unicorn.

2 Draw the lower part of the body.

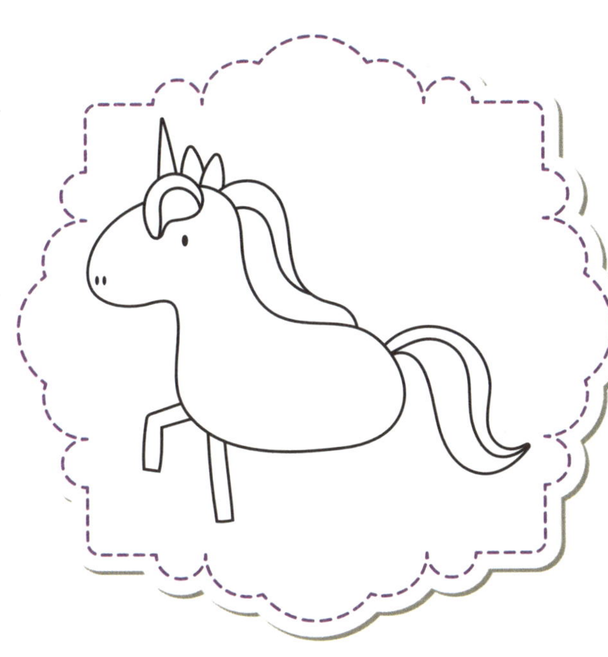

3 Draw the horns, hair, tail and front two legs of the animal.

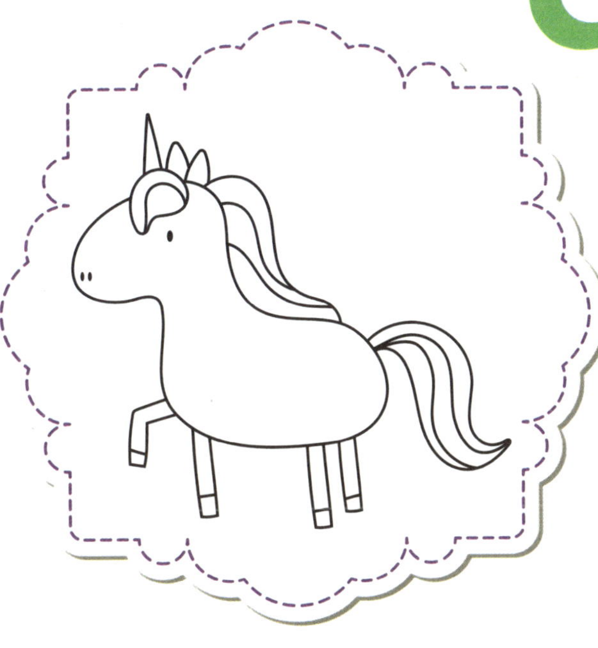

4 Draw the hind legs and draw more lines to make the hair and tail. Colour to complete.

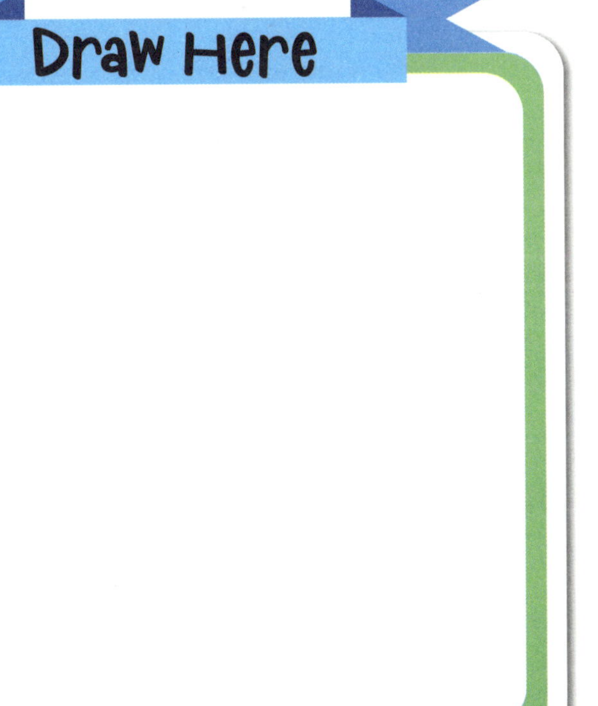

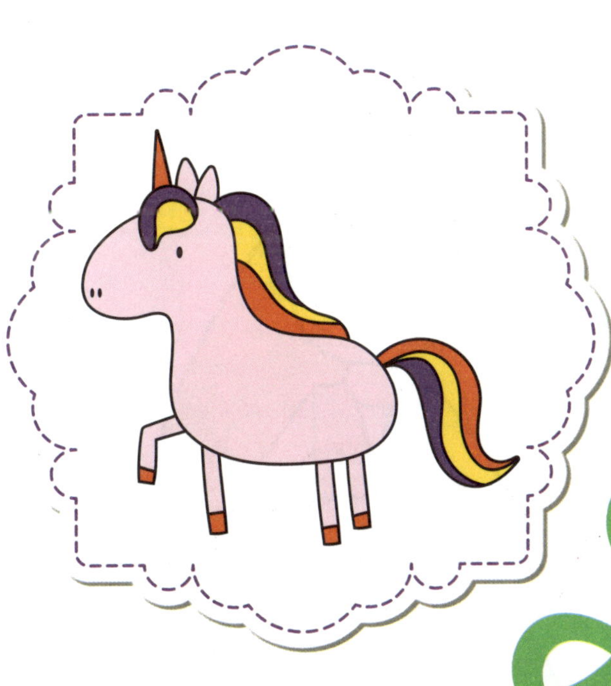

QUEEN

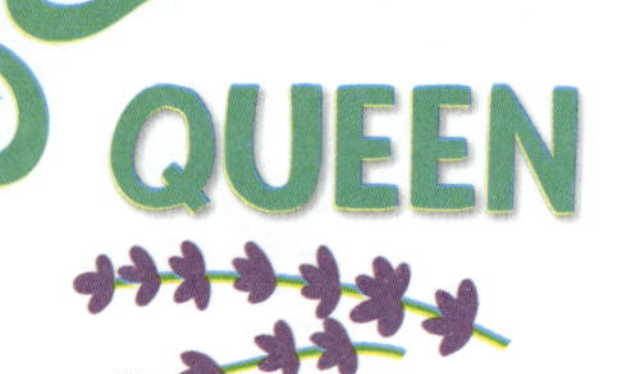

This is a queen. She is the wife of a king.

1 Draw the face, eyes and mouth of the queen.

2 Draw her torso and skirt, ears and crown.

3 Draw her hair, hands and dress and colour it as shown.

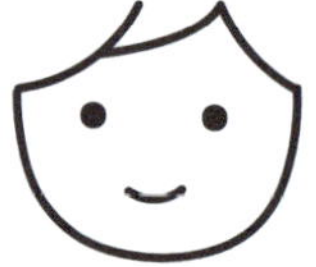

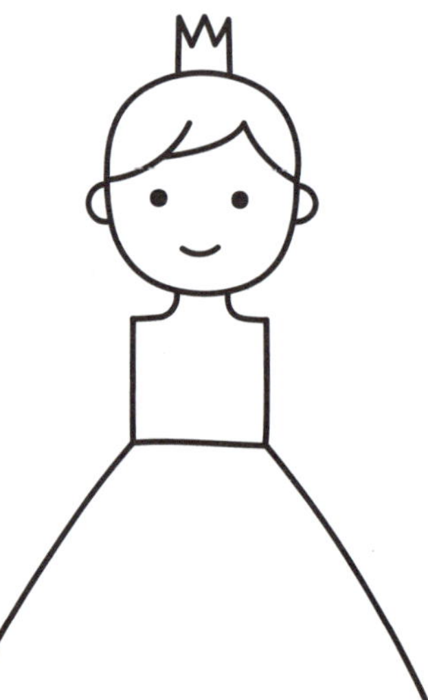

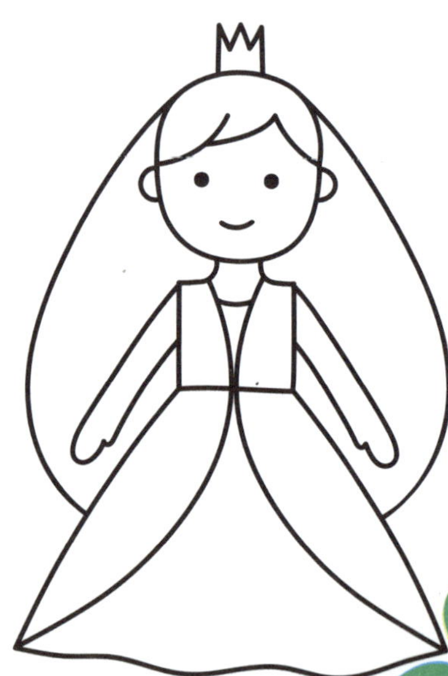

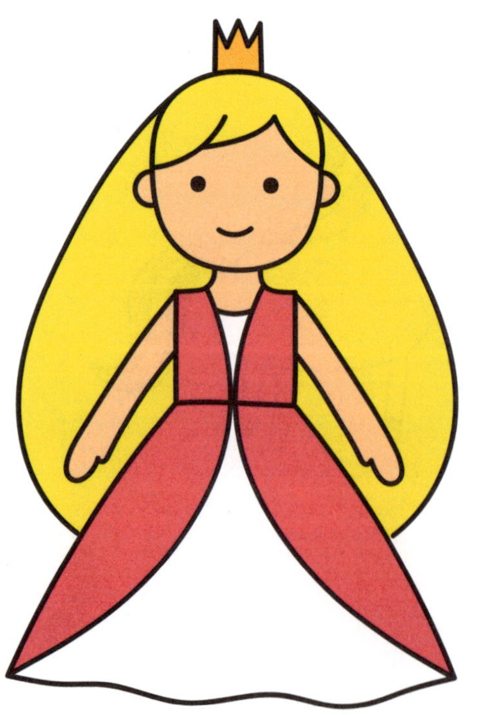

Draw Here